TALES of SOLUTIONS

Also by Insoo Kim Berg:

Building Solutions in Child Protective Services
(with Susan Kelly)
Family-Based Services: A Solution-Focused Approach
*The Miracle Method: A Radically New Approach to
Problem Drinking*
(with Scott D. Miller)
*Solutions Step by Step: A Substance Abuse Treatment
Manual*
(with Norman H. Reuss)
*Working with the Problem Drinker: A Solution-Focused
Approach*
(with Scott D. Miller)

Also by Yvonne Dolan:

*One Small Step: Moving Beyond Trauma and
Therapy to a Life of Joy*

*A Path With a Heart: Ericksonian Utilization with
Resistant and Chronic Clients*

*Resolving Sexual Abuse: Solution-Focused Therapy
and Ericksonian Hypnosis for
Adult Survivors*
(Norton)

A NORTON PROFESSIONAL BOOK

TALES of SOLUTIONS

A Collection of
Hope-inspiring
Stories

INSOO KIM BERG
&
YVONNE DOLAN

W. W. Norton & Company
New York • London

For information about permission to reproduce
selections from this book, write to
Permissions, W. W. Norton & Company, Inc.,
500 Fifth Avenue, New York, NY 10110

Composition by PRD Group
Manufacturing by Haddon Craftsmen

Library of Congress Cataloging-in-Publication Data

Berg, Insoo Kim
    Tales of solutions: a collection of hope-inspiring stories /
Insoo Kim Berg and Yvonne Dolan.
        p.   cm.—(A Norton professional book)
    Includes bibliographical references and index.
    ISBN 0-393-70320-7
    1. Solution-focused therapy—Case studies. I. Dolan, Yvonne M.,
1951-II. Title. III. Series.

RC489.S65 B47 2001
616.89'14—dc21   00-050109

W. W. Norton & Company, Inc., 500 Fifth Avenue,
New York, N.Y. 10110
www.wwnorton.com
W. W. Norton & Company, Ltd., 10 Coptic Street, London WC1A 1PU

1 2 3 4 5 6 7 8 9 0

To Steve de Shazer,
my best friend and colleague.
Love, IKB.

To Harry W. Taylor,
miracles do happen.
Love, YD.

CONTENTS

ACKNOWLEDGMENTS

In collecting these tales, we experienced firsthand the graciousness of our gifted and resourceful colleagues from all over the world who generously took the time to tell us the remarkable stories of their work with courageous and inspiring clients. Even though the book is finished, their stories continue to inspire us. We personally thank each person whose work touched our lives.

There were numerous other equally inspiring stories that we could not fit into this volume, but we thank each and every one of those contributors for their time. We were especially fortunate to receive the support of C. J. Kim, who helped us with the technical side of numerous file transfers and held our hands in times of panic over lost files; Sarah Berg helped us stay in touch and on top of mountains of papers and intractable attachments. We cannot thank enough our editors—Susan Munro, Regina Dahlgren Ardini, and Christine Habermaas—for their gentle questions and suggestions. Lastly, but definitely not least, I (YD) want to say a special thank you to Charlie Johnson for his ongoing encouragement throughout the project.

Insoo Kim Berg, Milwaukee
Yvonne Dolan, Denver

INTRODUCTION:
SPINNING STRAW INTO GOLD

The idea for this book came on a cold, snowy December night when we were teaching in Seoul, Korea. We were commiserating about a dilemma: Many of our most talented solution-focused colleagues never write about their work, and the therapy world misses out. In our workshops throughout the U.S., Canada, Europe, South America, and the Pacific Rim, we constantly hear tales of clients and therapists achieving remarkable results despite (or sometimes perhaps in reaction to) seemingly impossible social, economic, and personal situations. Often the therapeutic outcomes in these cases surprised both the client and the therapist. As we began to collect these real-life stories, we were reminded of the childhood fairy tale *Rumpelstiltskin,* in which the protagonist surprises everyone, herself included, by achieving something she thought impossible: spinning straw into gold. In a sense, that is exactly what the therapists and clients in this collection of tales have done.

STORIES THAT SHAPE OUR LIVES

We all have memorable cases or clients that shaped our careers or steered us in a certain direction. After more than 30 years, I (IKB) still remember Mrs. Fuller, a middle-aged woman who was very distraught. Being fairly new to the field of psychotherapy, I was eager to help anyone who appeared in my office. They were usually women in those days. Deadly serious in my desire to be helpful and professional, I was wearing my "dress for success" suit, high heels, and a string of pearls.

Between occasional tears and sighs, Mrs. Fuller explained that her husband of 27 years had recently lost control of his temper. For the first time in their long marriage he had slapped her across her face. She was rightfully upset and indignant about it. I was shocked, however, by what she said after she had described the details of the event. She began repeatedly blaming herself for not having known that her husband was going to be the kind of man who would hit a woman! She muttered to herself, "I should have known. I should have known he was going to turn out to be such a weak man that he was going to do this to me."

I thought that this was a rather strange thing to say for someone who had been slapped across the face for the very first time, so I leaned forward and asked, "Mrs. Fuller, what do you mean?" She explained that she still vividly remembered the first Monday after their return from their honeymoon. Her husband had dressed for work, but instead of walking out the door as she expected him to, he abruptly sat down on the bed, choked up, and, to her horror, began to weep.

Worried, she sat down next to him and gently asked, "What's the matter, honey?" This brought more sobs and tears. Then he explained that he was overwhelmed by the responsibility of supporting a wife who deserved to be supported well (most married women were homemakers in those days). Between more sobs, he said he was overcome with worry that he couldn't support her well enough because her parents were better off financially than his family.

Mrs. Fuller explained that she had been so touched by her husband's love for her and his desire to take care of her that she put her arms around him and reassured him that she did not have to live in luxury as long as they were happy together. After a while, her husband calmed down and went to work. I thought that it was a rather touching story, but I was a bit confused about how this tender episode related to her current thinking that she should have known what kind of a husband he would turn out to be. I asked her to explain. Without missing a beat, Mrs. Fuller said that she now realized she should have seen that he was a weakling who was scared of going to work and who would eventually end up slapping his wife around! I was stunned.

Then I realized that Mrs. Fuller was spinning a new yarn out of the same event she had viewed so differently in the past. Almost within the same breath, she revised her "gold thread" story of tender, loving moments into the "straw" tale of a weak, spineless man. This was my first glimpse of how all of us revise our history. Each retelling of the story changes and reshapes it a little bit.

Of course, I have since met many clients who retell their family backgrounds and the events in their lives. Gradually, I have come to realize that therapeutic phenomena such as "insight," "interpretation," and "reframing" are nothing more than retelling and thereby recreating stories.

We believe all therapeutic endeavors involve the retelling and reviewing of one's life, for it is through doing these activities that one experiences oneself as changing. The ability and willingness to rewrite our life stories makes it possible to shape, reshape, renegotiate, and change relationships in our lives. This makes it possible for us to fall in and out of love, marry, divorce, move onto new relationships, heal past hurt, and rebuild trusting relationships. I'm sure you have listened to friends, relatives, neighbors, and clients describe in warm, tender, enthusiastic words the person they fell in love with not many years ago. Later, when they are leaving the relationship, they describe the same person with very different words. It can be hard to believe they are describing the same person they once held so dear. This happens not only with love relationships, but also with friendships and business or political relationships.

On the other hand, we also come across clients, friends, or colleagues who are unable to change the story of a relationship, even after the first of many violent encounters. We tend to describe these people as "unrealistic," "frozen in time," "stuck in their fantasy," or even "pathological." We try to convince them to change their story or perception of the events.

We don't believe that how one tells one's story is a matter of being honest or dishonest. Rather, storytelling is a wonderful linguistic way that humans "spin straw into gold" and vice versa. This phenomenon goes on all the time, every day, all over the world, in every language. Of course, the more we repeat the same story, the more it becomes convincing. The more detailed the story, the more realistic it seems.

The "fish story" is a classic example of how stories evolve in the process of their retelling. The more times the fisherman repeats the story of "the fish that got away," the bigger the fish becomes. Personal and public accounts of history get revised all the time, depending on the motivation of the storyteller. There are no historical facts that have been written in stone and remain untouched over time. Naturally, this is also true of personal accounts of one's childhood. That is why siblings' accounts of their childhood, their parents, and the family "legend" can vary significantly.

As psychotherapists, we actively participate in the retelling of our clients' stories. In fact, we can describe our everyday work as exactly that of helping people revise and retell their stories in a manner that will help them move forward. While many approaches to therapy involve helping clients tell their stories, a distinguishing principle of the solution-focused approach is that the therapist empowers clients to retell their stories based upon their goals, rather than basing their goals upon their stories.

WHAT YOU CAN EXPECT FROM THIS BOOK

While the sophisticated practitioner will glean a deeper understanding of applications of solution-focused therapy in complex and difficult situations, readers who are new to the concepts will become better acquainted with this unique way of working. We have deliberately refrained from using the words *postmodernism, post-structuralism, social constructionism,* and a host of other phrases that we believe too often befuddle rather than clarify. Instead, we use these wonderful stories from across the globe to demonstrate how solution-focused therapy works in clinical practice and how seemingly small actions can yield big changes in people's lives. We also examine the more advanced technical questions that are likely to come up after you have read the various tales.

Although we have changed the clients' names and other details to protect confidentiality, we have attempted to preserve the therapists' original wording.

TALES of SOLUTIONS

Chapter 1

THE PRAGMATICS OF HOPE AND RESPECT: AN OVERVIEW OF THE SOLUTION-FOCUSED APPROACH

The stories in this book have been provided by therapists who use the solution-focused brief-therapy (SFBT) approach, a therapy model that is gaining worldwide attention and popularity because of its inherently respectful approach. Therapists who work from the SFBT model actively and consistently demonstrate respect for their clients by asking questions designed to value what the client wants and by both acknowledging and incorporating the client's past successes into the therapy process.

If we had to define the SFBT approach in one sentence without talking about philosophy or techniques, we would describe it as "the pragmatics of hope and respect." Rather than focusing on deficits, SFBT therapists view clients as competent and in possession of resources. SFBT therapists do not attempt to educate or "enlighten" clients; instead, they prefer to view clients as having positive rather than negative intentions. Completely accepting of the client's view, the SFBT therapist uses the client's perceptions as valuable resources to help create the change the client desires.

THE DEVELOPMENT OF THE SFBT APPROACH

As a treatment model, SFBT was originally developed in rebellion against traditional psychotherapeutic premises about people, problems of living, and the solutions to those problems. Not surprisingly, this model holds nontraditional views about how changes occur and the role of the therapist in relation to change. These differences have resulted in an effective and efficient use of two of the modern world's most valuable and limited resources: time and money.

Originally the product of a team effort, SFBT has evolved into its present form over the past 30 years. The original setting and composition of the team had a profound influence on the development of SFBT. The birthplace of the approach, Milwaukee, is a midsized American city located north of Chicago. The city's beginnings are rooted in its original Native American inhabitants, along with German and Polish immigrants. Although Milwaukee has had its share of tumultuous change, the people who live there have a reputation of being down-to-earth and hardworking, with a no-nonsense approach to enduring harsh winters and dealing with life in general.

The team members came from a variety of academic disciplines, including medicine, psychology, social work, education, sociology, philosophy, linguistics, and even biology and engineering. As lives changed, various team members came and went. Throughout the development of SFBT, the two people who endured and remained most committed to developing the model into its present form were Steve de Shazer and Insoo Kim Berg. Together, Berg and de Shazer have become the primary innovators and spokespersons for this worldwide "movement."

In addition, a number of practitioners, thinkers, teachers, and researchers have experimented with using the approach with diverse populations and in far-ranging situations, including psychiatric settings, schools, prisons, group homes, private homes, business environments, and homeless shelters or the streets. Populations that have benefited from SFBT include (to name only a few) parents, parents of drug-affected babies, the elderly, people who are dying of AIDS, crime victims, substance abusers, the unemployed, business people, and government agencies.

Frequently described as an approach that requires clinicians to "think out of the box," SFBT was developed inductively rather than deductively. The result is an eminently respectful approach that vastly expands the view of health beyond the simple classifications of "pathological" or "unhealthy." Even though SFBT recognizes, accepts, and works with the hierarchical nature of the therapist/client relationship, the SFBT therapist's relationship with clients is markedly more egalitarian and democratic than authoritarian.

You will notice that the therapists in the stories throughout this book rarely make judgments about what clients want and desire. Instead, they ask a series of questions that expand rather than limit the client's options. This is described as "leading from one step behind" (Cantwell & Holmes, 1994). As these words imply, SFBT therapists do not shy away from leading; however, rather than pushing, cajoling, or pulling their clients in certain directions, they lead from behind. From this position, the therapist gently "taps the client on the shoulder" and asks whether she noticed the beautiful sunset in the sky or that tiny wild flower swaying in the breeze. These "taps on the shoulder" are the questions that the therapist asks in order to stimulate a fresh look at the same old picture. What the client ultimately chooses to do with this fresh view of the sunset or a wild flower is up to her but making this choice possible for the client is very important. SFBT therapists have also found that certain ways of phrasing therapeutic questions produce better answers, and, as you will learn later in this chapter, there are certain prescribed questions.

CREATING AND NEGOTIATING THE FUTURE

SFBT therapists believe that the future is both created and negotiable. This means that we are not slaves of our past history and we need not view our future as predetermined by past experience or family history. Of course, we acknowledge that one's way of doing things is shaped by one's family, culture, and ethnic heritage, but beyond this, what kind of person you want to become can be created and negotiated.

Thus, the focus is on asking clients what kind of future they want and how that future will fit with their ideas of what they want to have in their lives. There is very little emphasis on the client's history—how miserable she has been or how much trauma he has suffered. The SFBT therapist views the client's future in a very optimistic, hopeful manner and tries to communicate this to the client.

This optimistic view is maintained even when reality seems to indicate the opposite. This has prompted some therapists to call us Pollyannas or other unflattering names. We accept this description, however, and are rather proud of the naivete that separates us from the mainstream. Our view is this: Considering all the misfortune that she and her village suffered, if Pollyanna did not have such a naively optimistic point of view, she could have become an alcoholic, a drug addict, or even committed suicide. In fact, her naively optimistic tendency saved her life and the entire village!

Some clients may tell you they need to "understand" their past before they can move on to their future. But it seems logical to say that, even without completely "understanding the past," the client has still managed to move on—that is, he or she has lived a life by going to work, going to school, getting married, having children, buying a house, and so on. Of course, I would not try to explain this to the client, because the client's desire is to "understand" the past. I believe most people, both professionals and laymen alike, believe that we *must* have insight into our past to achieve something, even if that something isn't perfectly clear.

Our view is that there are multiple ways to "understand the past" or interpret past events. Our job is to help the client find the most useful and helpful way to interpret or make meaning of the past. No matter how the client chooses to do this, we should be interested in how this new "understanding" will influence his or her decision about how to live in the future. Therefore, questions like the following are helpful:

- "I can understand you want to make sense of this terrible thing that happened to you when you were young. So, suppose that eventually you *do* get to understand your past to your satisfaction—what will you do then that you are not doing right now?"
- "Suppose you could understand your past right now. What difference would it make for you?"

The more we talk about "differences," the more we emphasize the changes the client will make.

SOLUTION BUILDING VS. PROBLEM SOLVING

According to DeJong and Berg (1998), solution-building thinking and activities are quite different from problem-solving thinking and activities (sometimes described as the "scientific" or "medical" model). Reduced to simple terms, problem solving can be understood as follows: First, information is gathered in order to identify the problem. This might include determining the history of the problem's onset and detailing the symptoms. Next comes speculation about the possible underlying causes of the problem. After this is analyzed in detail, the treatment of choice is identified. Finally, a treatment plan that will "resolve" or ameliorate the problem is prescribed and put into effect.

In contrast to problem solving, solution building as practiced in SFBT begins with clients' descriptions of how they want their lives to be different. It can be understood as beginning with the end of the story rather than the beginning of the problems. Because most of us are accustomed to being preoccupied with what we want to eliminate rather than create in our lives, it is not surprising that both clinicians and clients often find that formulating sustainable goals is more difficult than they anticipated.

The second step of solution building is to search for evidence or instances in which clients have experienced or are already experiencing bits and pieces of the desired life they identified in step one. At this point we further part company from the traditional therapeutic models. Usually we accomplish the next step by asking the "miracle question."

THE MIRACLE QUESTION: BORN OUT
OF DESPERATION

The miracle question is a technique that empowers clients to generate and describe their preferred outcomes—that is, what they want to have happen in their life as a result of therapy. The origin of this technique is itself an interesting story. In the mid-'80s I (IKB) was talking with a very tired, depressed, suicidal mother who described herself as having nothing right going on in her life. Her four children were out of control and the school was complaining almost daily about their behavior. Her alcoholic husband had difficulty keeping a job longer than six months, and she had worked herself into a state of exhaustion, with no relief in sight.

When I asked in my optimistic tone, "So what do you suppose needs to come out of this meeting today so that you can say that it was worth your while?" she looked at me, heaved a big sigh, and said sadly, "I am not sure that anything can be done about my life. I don't mean to be rude, but I'm not even sure why I'm talking to you because I'm not sure if anything can be done."

Rather discouraged by this pessimistic answer and not knowing what to say, I sat silently for a few moments. Then the mother casually added, "Unless you have a miracle." Of course, I did not have a miracle. But not knowing what else to say under the circumstances of such heavy hopelessness, I felt I had to follow up on this mother's idea of a miracle. So I gently asked in a soft voice, "Well, suppose there was a miracle, what would be different for you?" As she began to answer, she perked up, making a long list of how life will be easier, beginning with her having more energy and feeling she could "go on" with her life of raising her children. She then proceeded to describe what would be different between herself and her alcoholic husband, and how each of the children would change, and so on.

You probably have heard your own clients say similar things, perhaps many times. But I think what made me take particular notice in this situation was that I was desperate enough to really pay attention to the client and then follow through with her idea. I was fascinated with her response and consequently I followed up on her ideas about how her life would change, along with her "impossible" children.

After much experimentation with various phrasings, we have come up with the current version of the miracle question, which is surprisingly applicable across a wide range of cultures, population demographics, and problem categories:

I am going to ask you a rather strange question. [pause] The strange question is this: [pause] After we talk, you will go back to your work (home, school) and you will do whatever you need to do the rest of today, such as taking care of the children, cooking dinner, watching TV, giving the children a bath, and so on. It will become time to go to bed. Everybody in your household is quiet, and you are sleeping in peace. In the middle of the night, a miracle happens *and the problem that prompted you to talk to me today is solved!* But because this happens while you are sleeping, you have no way of knowing that there was an overnight miracle that solved the problem. [pause] So, when you wake up tomorrow morning, what might be the small change that will make you say to yourself, "Wow, something must have happened—the problem is gone!"

If you carefully observe clients' reactions to the miracle question, you'll notice that they go through various observable changes: They may appear to direct their attention inward as their body relaxes. Often the pupils of their eyes become dilated and their eyelids flutter as they consider the question. Some begin to smile as they become absorbed in the experience. Therapists familiar with the trance states elicited and utilized in Ericksonian hypnotherapy will notice that clients in SFBT therapy initially evidence a similar trancelike response when asked the miracle question.

Clients' most common immediate response to the miracle question after they have considered it is "I don't know." When this happens, don't worry that they have not understood the question or that they are unable to think of a solution. Instead, pause comfortably for a few moments, allowing them a generous amount of time to compose themselves and organize their thoughts. This little pause is a small but crucial detail. Depending on the client's personality and style, it may take several seconds or a few minutes to reorient from the trance state and begin formulating an answer to the question.

Over the years we have become quite fascinated by the way many clients preface especially heartfelt and important statements with the words "I don't know." We have learned to listen very carefully when a client says "I don't know" in a thoughtful, tentative tone. Typically those words are followed by a self-disclosing statement that indicates a major shift in the way they are thinking about their life. For example, we have observed that clients often preface a new idea they are considering (e.g., starting school, leaving an abusive partner, finding a job, or taking charge of their life in some other significant way) with "I don't know."

When I (YD) first observed this phenomenon, I thought it might be characteristic only of women who had been abused, the population with which I was working at the time. It seemed logical that someone who had been abused might doubt her perceptions and therefore use "I don't know" as a disclaimer. Then I noticed that many men did it too, and not only people who had suffered abuse or trauma. Later I wondered if it was a cultural nuance particular to the midwestern part of the U.S. where I was practicing. But then I began seeing clients from many different cultures within and outside the U.S., and I realized it was characteristic of them as well.

Over time, I've learned that when clients respond to the miracle question with "I don't know" before pausing and continuing, I can expect them to confide new and intimate information about themselves. Furthermore, they are using the disclaimer "I don't know" as a linguistic marker that allows them more freedom in their thinking. "I don't know" implies that the words that they are about to utter are not certainties. Consequently, they can summon the courage to voice previously unspoken hopes and dreams— what Irish songwriter Van Morrison so evocatively calls the "inarticulate speech of the heart." It all begins with asking the seemingly simple miracle question.

Once the client has answered the miracle question, the therapist's next task is to build on this small beginning of the pictured solution by asking for increasingly detailed descriptions of how the client's life will be better. Scaling is an important tool for empowering the client to create a vivid, detailed representation of the solution.

SCALING QUESTIONS

The human urge to measure, count, compare, chart, and figure out where one stands in relation to something else seems limitless. Even grandparents do this with their tiny grandchildren. Grandmother extends her hands parallel to each other and lovingly asks her little grandchild, "How much do you love Grandma—*this* much or [widening the space between her hands a little more] *this* much?" It seems the toddler understands the difference between the widening and narrowing of her grandmother's hands, because she responds appropriately to please Grandma.

We think of scaling as an anchoring tool that allows clients to measure, assess, and evaluate their own situations. It helps them visualize the next level in their progress and identify what additional effort they may have to put out. In many of the stories in this book, therapists ask clients this basic scaling question:

"On a scale of 0 to 10, where 10 means you feel that life is going as well as it could be and 0 means you feel like this is the worst day of your life, where would you say you are in relation to 10 right now?"

Of course, there are numerous ways of asking clients to measure and compare their situation. You will encounter these variations throughout the book, and you may think of different ways of applying them to your own situation. For example, when I (YD) work with clients who dislike numbers, we sometimes use symbols. A six-year-old girl who was feeling sad and wanted to feel better drew a frowning face to the left of a horizontal line, and then a happy face at the other end. She quickly related her "mood" scale to a game she played at home that involved moving a marker across a board to reach a goal at the other end. Using the structure of the scale, she was able to identify some activities that would help her begin to feel a little better, such as talking on the telephone to her father, who had recently moved out of the house.

Affective states can be acknowledged and respectfully assessed through scaling questions, which also help clients identify what they can do to influence or alter those states, if that is desired or necessary. A special advantage of scaling questions for people in emotional distress is that the question itself communicates the message that clients are more than just their emotional states. This helps clients begin to create a more tenable perspective for feelings that would otherwise be so overwhelming as to be debilitating or too scary to acknowledge aloud. The question itself provides a structure for clients to figure out where they are in relation to the intensity of the emotion without necessarily implying that they need to change or alter their emotional state. For example, since I (YD) specialize in working with posttraumatic stress disorders, I often see clients who have very recently experienced a trauma. Many times, they voice the fear that they will "always feel this bad." Asking them to imagine what would help them feel even the tiniest bit better allows clients to communicate what they need. Furthermore, the question itself implicitly communicates the much-needed reassurance that the pain will not always stay this bad.

EXCEPTIONS

One of the premises of SFBT is the idea that no problem happens all of the time—that is, there are exceptions, times when the problem does not occur. This idea came to the Milwaukee team in the late '70s and became the lightning rod for our innovative approach. If clients already have an exception—that is, a past success—why not get them to repeat these successes until they are satisfied with the way their life is going?

The discovery of exceptions led to immediate change in the tone of our sessions: client/therapist conversations became hopeful and optimistic. By asking about times when the problem doesn't occur or is less pronounced, the therapist identifies past exceptions that the client can then utilize as resources for change.

COMPLIMENTS AS INTERVENTION

Compliments are an integral part of SFBT sessions, regardless of the number of sessions. It is our way of acknowledging that there are a number of things going well in the midst of clients' troubled lives—that even though everything seems dismal to them, there are lots of little successes, good things they have done (or currently doing), and positive intentions, even if things haven't panned out as they intended.

Client responses to compliments are varied and fascinating. Of course, the most common response is to relax, breathe a deep sigh of relief, nod at every word the therapist says, and become tearful. Clients often add validating information, like the mother who said, "You don't know half of what I've been through during the last five years" when I commented on how much she had bravely struggled through. Occasionally a client will be stunned and become immobilized in response to a compliment. We believe that compliments help support clients who may not know that it is quite normal for someone who has lost a loved one to be depressed, or for a wife who just discovered that her husband betrayed their "marriage vows in front of God," as one woman described it, to be angry.

We believe that validating and acknowledging what clients are doing right and how difficult their problems are gives them permission to change and allows them to chart a new course of action. It also seems to allow them to think about how to make their lives more satisfying for them and others.

The following example highlights the use of compliments as an intervention. You will recognize how freeing it seems for people, restoring their sense of dignity and making them feel certain about what they want. Compliments are obviously positive but they do not have to be obvious in highlighting the client's accomplishments or extraordinary efforts. The following compliment intervention comes from our colleague Gale Miller, who teaches medical residents how to interview patients effectively:

> Doctor: Do you smoke?
> Patient: I used to, but I quit four years ago.
> Doctor: That's great. Why did you decide to quit?

Another example:

> Doctor: Do you smoke?
> Patient: I used to, but I quit four years ago.
> Doctor: That's great. How did you do it?

The minor change in wording makes a big difference. "How" questions tend to emphasize clients' resourcefulness and ingenuity, while "why" questions challenge clients' motivations. SFBT utilizes "how" questions because they implicitly compliment the client.

THE TREATMENT PROCESS:
THE NUTS AND BOLTS OF THERAPY

There are some steps to making therapy shorter and more effective. However, we want to remind you that a therapy session is a very complex activity and many subtle and not so subtle things happen during a single hour, both verbal and nonverbal. Here we simply highlight the most important events that occur that set the tone for the session. In the first session:

1. Ask your client, "What needs to happen that will tell you that today's meeting has been useful?" Rather than talking about clients' problems, ask, as soon as it becomes reasonable, what kind of outcome will tell them that this session was useful and helpful. Negotiating termination criteria implies that there is an end to their suffering.

2. As the client details the picture of the solution, the therapist should ask questions about exceptions. These questions uncover the client's previous successes in mastering problems. If the answer to the exception question is "yes," find out the details of "how" the client managed to change his or her ordinary behavior. For example: "Tell me about the most recent time when you could have pulled up the covers and stayed in bed all day, but somehow you managed to force yourself out of bed." Note the exact wording of this question, which presupposes that the client successfully overcame the temptation to stay in bed and remain depressed. The fact that this client is sitting (or standing) in front of the therapist and talking means somehow she managed to get out of bed that morning. This kind of inquiry helps clients change their perceptions. Your client may feel overwhelmed by life 24 hours a day, 7 days a week, but when the facts prove otherwise, she will adjust her perception accordingly. Exceptions to problems not only highlight client competencies, however small, but also point to the direction from where the solution may come.

3. Ask the miracle question. Even though you may have a good idea for a solution, answering the miracle question helps clients realize that they have lots of good ideas about how they want life to be different. Imagining the details of the miracle provides clients with many practical ideas about how to enact positive change. Make sure that the miracles involve all the important people in the client's life—her child, her best friend, the most supportive person she knows—and how they might respond to her first problem-free day, immediately after the miracle. The beauty of the miracle question is that the ideas for solution all come from the client and are based on the past experiences of the client, not the therapist. Be prepared to hear some very touching solutions, such as the mother who answered that the first thing she would do would be to "comb her little daughter's hair" before the daughter went off to school. It seemed like such a small and insignificant idea until the therapist asked the mother what this would mean to her and she answered that it would mean that she would not have done cocaine the night before as usual but that she would be able to get up with her daughter instead of sleeping all day following her night of doing drugs.

4. Find out when the client has recently experienced even a little bit of the miracle day. This is crucial, because if a client has had even a half day of mastery over problems, he or she has the potential to extend the half day into a whole day, or into two days, and so on. Many beginning SFBT therapists report that it is here that they begin to lose focus, because clients frequently minimize their small successes or counter their own miracles by reverting to "problem talk." When this happens, refocus the conversation on the successful strategies the client came up with and then stay with this as long as you can. Again, ask about what other important people in the client's life would say if they were explaining how the client accomplished this small success.

5. When you feel like you have sufficiently covered the exceptions, you can move into asking about the confidence scale. It is always a good idea to explain the parameters of what 1 stands for and what 10 stands for, so that the client does not fly off into theoretical numerical space. Even when you are specific about what the numbers stand for, some clients will say things like, "I'm at 132 today!"

6. When the client is confident that he or she can repeat the successful strategies, the conversation should shift to "What will it take to make that solution happen again?" Once more, having the client provide the rich details of the solution is very important because it works as a type of dress rehearsal.

7. At the end of the session, the therapist generally summarizes what he or she heard from the client about areas of competence, successes, positive intentions, and how the client overcame the odds against making it. This of course naturally calls for the therapist to give the client a compliment. This compliment is then followed by a suggestion for homework. Most SFBT homework suggestions are along the lines of "do more of what works."

The second session usually begins with "What's better, even a little bit?" Notice that the sentence structure assumes that something is better and that the therapist is interested in finding out about it. (Contrast this with a question like, "How are things going?" or "Is anything better since we met last time?") As you can see, the question is designed to elicit some gain the client has made between the first meeting and the second. Once the success, however small, is identified, the conversation will naturally follow the details of who did what, when, where, and how. Then the task becomes one of maintaining the momentum of success and building success upon success until the scaling questions indicate that the client is satisfied with the progress of solution building, at which point he or she may decide to end the therapy.

This is a necessarily brief description of what happens in the majority of SFBT cases; of course, it is difficult to describe the rich and wonderful details of all the unexpected turns and twists that occur when we are dealing with real life and the wise and foolish things we humans do. But you can see that the focus is on the client's living a satisfying life outside the therapy room in the real world, rather than on getting along with the therapist inside the secure and comfortable office, talking theoretically about life instead of actually living it. It seems like a commonsense, logical, reasonable, and simple thing to do but it's a lot harder to do. "Simple" is not easy and it takes discipline to stay simple.

FOCUSING ON LIVING A REAL LIFE WITHIN
A SOCIAL CONTEXT: RELATIONSHIP QUESTIONS

Positive relationships between clients and therapists are created right from the beginning in SFBT. It is the therapist's responsibility to learn as much as possible about a client's thought process, worldview, and orientation to life and then join in on these views. The therapist must work within the client's frame of mind, not try to change it. Therefore, we assume that as therapists we are obligated to immediately place ourselves on the side of the clients, certainly not opposite them. We have a strong commitment to making sure that we are always working *with* the client.

Frequently, it is the rich details of real-life events that offer us valuable information about who and what is important to the client. We believe this focus on clients' important relationships also implies that the therapy will be brief and that our task is to assist them in enriching their lives in practical ways. Thus, the constant focus of the client-therapist conversation should be on the client's life outside the therapy room. You will hear the SFBT therapist asking questions like these:

- What do you suppose your wife would say if she were to explain how you have been helpful to her? Or, what would your wife say about how she would like you to be helpful?
- How would she know that a miracle occurred overnight and your drinking problem is solved without your telling her that?
- What would your children notice is different about you that tells them they no longer have to worry about your health (depression, anger, anxiety, temper, etc.)?
- How would your children be different if you and your husband were able to talk to each other without yelling and screaming? What would they say if they were to explain how helpful it would be for them?
- What would your best friend tell me if he or she were to explain how you keep going in the midst of all these terrible things?
- What have you noticed is different about your family that tells you they are relieved to have you feeling better?

Questions that place the client in real-life situations shows the client that we are interested in his or her real-life relationships with a significant person or people. Notice also that these questions force clients to step out of themselves and observe themselves through the eyes of those who are close to them. This was done in a unique and creative way in the following story.

A Letter to His Father
Contributed by Sverre Barth, M.D., Oslo, Norway

Per, a good-looking, 26-year-old man, came to see me because of his long-standing problems with writing. Hunched over and list-less, he seemed like he was afraid to look up at the sky and enjoy the bright day. His lifelong ambition had been to become a lawyer, and he had painstakingly studied to pass many examinations in schools for many years. Now he was facing the bar exam, and he was terrified of failing.

I asked when this problem had started. He replied that it had begun when he was seven years old. Startled at the early onset of the problem, I asked whether that was the age when children start to learn to write in school. Per replied that indeed his problem be-gan when he started to learn to write. No matter how hard he tried to improve, his writing had remained clumsy all his life. In spite of numerous psychiatric treatments and a rather successful aca-demic career, Per felt he had always been a failure.

Per also explained that his highly successful father had always told him he would "never amount to anything." This had remained in his mind even after his father's death several years ago. Per de-scribed his father's oppressive haranguing and the terror he felt whenever he thought about him. Important tests triggered a para-lyzing fear of failure for him.

I referred Per to a neurologist, who diagnosed him with dyslexia. Armed with this diagnosis, Per was able to secure a special com-puter and financial and other assistance from the government. He also hired a secretary to take notes and organize his writings.

When the exam date came closer, Per became convinced that he was "not going to make it." In response, I asked him, "What would help your father in his grave to know that he had been wrong about you? How could you convince your father that even he was capable of making a mistake?" Per was perplexed and said he had no idea.

So I said that this was one of those situations in life where action, not just talking, was needed. I offered the following suggestion: Per was to go to his father's grave with a piece of paper, a pen, a camera, and a candle. He was to light the candle and place it on the grave with a note that said, "Forgive me, Father. I am going to pass the exam this time." Per would then take a picture of his father's grave and return to the city. Soon after Per left the session, he called to tell me he was modifying my suggestion. Instead of going to the village where his father's grave was, Per decided to select a spot in King's Castle Park, which overlooks the Oslo harbor, light a candle, and place the note in front of the candle. He then would take a picture and bury the note.

As you may have guessed, Per passed the bar exam and is now practicing law outside of Oslo.

Realizing that Per has had numerous therapies designed to resolve the oppressive influence of his father without much success, Barth wisely decided that his patient needed an immediate experience of success in a real-life situation—his bar examination—and gave a suggestion designed to put a closure to his father's unrelenting message of doom. The ritual is designed to respectfully put his father into his grave; it is not designed out of anger. We are amused and delighted by how Per decided to modify the therapist's suggestions by choosing King's Castle, a beautiful spot overlooking Oslo harbor, to say farewell to his father's message of doom. We also like the way Barth offered some practical help for his dyslexia, in addition to his symbolic gestures. Those who use SFBT are known to use whatever works, a very pragmatic and realistic approach.

USING THERAPY AS A DRESS REHEARSAL: WORKING WITH VICTIMS OF ABUSE

The optimism of the SFBT approach makes it ideally suited as a dress rehearsal in which clients can build solutions in a positive, practical way. This is especially true with victims of abuse and other trauma. One of the first things that attracted me (YD) to SFBT was the fact that it provided a virtual corrective experience for victims. I have spent the past twenty-some years working with people who have been physically, emotionally, or sexually abused and suffered other forms of trauma. Regardless of the kind of abuse they suffered, the victims typically describe the experience as one in which they were disrespected and treated like an object with no value. The abuser either ignored or discounted the victim's feelings of distress. Even if the victim subsequently attempted to confront the abuser, the abuser usually discounted the victim's perceptions.

Thus, besides suffering the event of abuse itself, victims usually come away with the idea that their perceptions and feelings are not valid or worthy of respect. Because they have been so violated by another human being, it is usually very difficult for a victim of abuse to trust a therapist enough to get help. Not surprisingly, the professional literature about treating victims of abuse and other forms of trauma is rampant with strategies designed to help therapists deal with the client's negative transference and reluctance to trust. Unfortunately, approaches in which the therapist determines the goal and course of treatment are all too likely to remind the client of those traumatic experiences in which someone else was in control of what was happening. Abusive relationships are usually characterized by someone more powerful than the victim determining what will happen in the interaction. No wonder trust issues come up when clients are subjected to the goals and agenda of the therapist (or to the protocol of the therapist's approach) rather than their own! Even worse, in some traditional clinical settings, clients who object to a discrepancy between what they want to have happen and what the therapist seems to want are given the pathologizing and implicitly pejorative label of "borderline."

If I decided to construct an interactive experience that was the exact opposite of the abuse experience, it would look remarkably like a SFBT interview. With the SFBT approach, the client's perceptions, feelings, and preferences are invited, valued, explored, and used to determine the direction and process of therapy. They are subsequently employed as the criterion for whether the therapy was successful. Furthermore, clients usually are given respectful compliments during or at the conclusion of each session.

All of this is, of course, in sharp contrast to the hurtful messages that occur in abuse. While SFBT compliments are often helpful in empowering clients to become more fully aware of their strengths and abilities, it may well be the *implicit* rather than explicit communication of the clients' worth that is most effective. People who have been abused often have experienced the painful discrepancy between what the abuser says and what the abuser does. SFBT therapists' consistent behavior of asking clients what they want and carefully listening to clients' ideas about the problem and potential solutions provides an immediate experience of validation and respect that is congruent with the compliments. During my sessions, I make a point of writing down anything clients are doing well (exceptions) to enhance the implicit message of validation. This tells them that what they are doing is significant, valuable, and literally noteworthy.

The next story illustrates how SFBT was used with a woman facing domestic abuse.

From Hopelessness to Independence
Contributed by Jacek Lelonkiewicz, Lodz, Poland

Thirty-two-year-old Beatrice came to see me after her friend read a newspaper article about the center where I worked and urged her to go. She was unsure, however, about her decision to come because she felt hopeless about changing her difficult situation.

Beatrice had been physically and emotionally abused by her husband for many years. Although only 34 years old, her husband was a very successful businessman and was considered a pillar of their community. Beatrice had been a very successful Olympic figure skater in the past, but had stopped skating competitively when she became pregnant. After the birth of her second child, she gave up skating altogether so she could stay at home with the children. Her husband's work kept him very busy, and she was often alone at home caring for the children. Throughout the seven years of their marriage, her husband had become increasingly critical of her and had started beating her. Twice she had been taken to the emergency room because of the severity of his beatings.

Beatrice felt hopeless about making him stop. She had tried to take him to court on two separate occasions, but his prominence and increasing influence in the community had given him powerful connections with the police, judges, and everyone at the top of the legal system, and he had used these connections to block her efforts. She now saw no possibility of getting help from the legal authorities. I agreed with Beatrice's perception of her difficulties, but I nevertheless asked, "Suppose that it would be possible to change the situation. What would be different?" She responded by saying that her goal was to live independently and happily. She answered the miracle question with a very clear and detailed description of how life would be different for her.

I then asked Beatrice to imagine a scale in which 10 represented life after the miracle and 0 represented things at their worst. She rated herself at a 2. I then asked, "If your husband were to become aggressive again, what would be the smallest step you could take to move forward on the scale?" She answered that instead of passively staying at home, she would do something active, such as volunteering to teach young children to skate, getting back to skating for fun and fitness, or helping other women less fortunate than herself. Most of all, she wanted to stay connected to her family and friends. This would raise her on the scale to a 4. When I asked her to scale her level of motivation, with 0 representing no motivation and 10 representing maximum motivation, she rated herself at a 5.

I complimented Beatrice on her intelligent ideas about her situation, her realism, and her ability to maintain hope, because having ideas means having hope. At the end of the session I gave her the first-session formula task (de Shazer, 1985) as homework: "Between now and the next session, notice the things in your life that you would like to continue."

When Beatrice returned for the second session, she said that she and her husband had argued and he had hit her. This time she went to the neighbors and called the police. Her husband assumed that nothing would come of it, but this time he was wrong. The police officer who responded to her call was not important enough to be acquainted with her husband, and, not knowing her husband was a powerful man in the community, the officer treated him as he would anyone else and arrested him.

Beatrice then went to the doctor for a physical exam, and she also confided in those family members and friends who had not known about the abuse. With the support of her friends, she decided to take her husband to court. I complimented Beatrice on knowing clearly what she wanted and on having supportive friends. I also advised her to continue to do more of what she had found to be helpful.

When Beatrice returned for her next session, her husband was being prosecuted. She had found a new place to live and had begun skating again.

EMOTIONS AND EMPATHY IN SFBT

In our combined experience of more than 50 years, we have observed many ways that SF therapists honor and respect the client's affective experience and significantly incorporate it into the therapeutic process. In our workshops we often hear the question: "What do you do when the client says that the most crucial aspect of the solution is that they would be feeling differently?" This kind of thinking seems to come from the idea that there are logical, sequential steps to "uncover" the layers of problems, like peeling the layers of an onion. Many clients also believe that they want to "get to the bottom" of the problem, believing that the true cause of the problem can be pinpointed. This kind of logical connection between the problem and its cause makes sense in other situations in life but doesn't always hold true for the human mind.

When clients say, "I have to feel better (or differently) in order to change some aspect of my thinking (or behavior)," they are actually making themselves feel more helpless: they are dependent upon having something *else* change before they take an active step to change themselves. This way of thinking is too limited and rigid. It also comes from the perception that somehow emotions are a separate entity, unconnected to behavior or thought. We believe that thoughts, behaviors, and emotions are intricately connected—for example, sometimes a client first feels a change and then acts on it; other times behavioral changes are followed by cognitive or emotional shifts.

Attaching words to emotions helps identify them, but such activities must be followed by cognitive and/or behavioral shifts to be useful. If the client defines the problem in terms of an emotional state and identifies the solution as a shift in that state, it is important to explore how the client is going to shift into that desired state. For example, the therapist could ask: "How will others be able to tell that you are feeling differently?" or "What difference will the feeling make—what will you do differently after your feeling has changed?" or "What would you look like on videotape after you are feeling differently?" If the answer is, "Nothing would be obvious on videotape or to anyone else," you can ask more about the experience of the feeling. A helpful question might be, "When in the past have you felt the way you want to feel now? What were you doing or telling yourself then?"

When the solution is identified as a shift in an emotional state, the therapist runs the risk of inadvertently sending the message that some feelings are "bad" and others "good." Furthermore, unless the therapist talks about emotions in response to the client's own spontaneous emotional expression, and from within the context of the client's current life, there is the danger of trivializing or marginalizing the client's immediate experience. Regardless of whether the therapist states it directly, the message that a client *must* talk explicitly about feelings in order to participate "correctly" in the therapeutic experience can be as limiting and tyrannizing for the client as the opposite assumption that talking about emotions is off-limits.

SFBT allows clients to determine whether it is useful and meaningful to talk about emotions based upon what they wish to have happen as a result of therapy. Ironically, it is perhaps this very latitude in the SFBT approach that helps the client experience an emotional climate in which it is safe to talk about feelings. People don't like to feel forced to talk about feelings any more than they like being forced to talk about anything else.

Perhaps because of the specificity of the questions associated with the SFBT model, people who have only a partial understanding of the approach sometimes worry that this way of working could be experienced as mechanistic or superficial. They wonder how the SFBT therapist communicates empathy and builds a relationship in which the client feels safe enough to tell us "where it hurts." In addition to providing a "positive emotional climate" (Lipchik, 1999), the SFBT interview creates an immediate and interactive "social context" (Miller & de Shazer, 2000) in which the client receives both explicit and implicit messages that their beliefs, perceptions, preferences, feelings, and ideas are legitimately valuable and useful. Feelings of empathy on the part of the therapist are, like other feelings, contextual.

Empathy is communicated to the client verbally and nonverbally, in subtle and not-so-subtle ways. The therapist can empathize with the client while helping her find solutions to a dilemma or, as the following dialogue shows, while looking for resources.

Peggy, a 35-year-old mother of two young children, and a part-time teacher, had just found out three days earlier that her husband of six years, Bob, had been having an affair for six months. During the interview, between tears, deep sighs, and rage at her husband, her affect swung between shame because her best friend suspected the affair but never told her, rage at the betrayal of their wedding vows, and distrust of her lying husband. She wondered whether she should throw Bob out of the house and force him to confess his betrayal to the world or to get a lawyer and file for divorce; there was a host of other options she couldn't decide on either. Peggy was feeling a wide range of emotion and very confused. Toward the end of the session, Peggy came up with the idea that she needed to get away from all the turmoil and confusion she had been experiencing for the past three days.

> *Peggy: I mean, if anybody's gonna leave that house permanently, it's gonna be him.*
> *Insoo: Okay. Makes sense.*
> *Peggy: No, I'm just talking about—I just need a little break. You know what I mean, I'm just talking about a short vacation; I'm not talking about divorce. No.*
> *Insoo: So you need a short break first. You need to get away for a short time first.*
> *Peggy: Yeah.*
> *Insoo: And then you will come back.*
> *Peggy: I've put too much . . .*

Insoo: Of course you have.

Peggy: You know, I planted 350 tulip bulbs in my garden.

Insoo: Oh.

Peggy: Last fall. You know, that's my house.

Insoo: Yeah. So what will tell you this is time to make the next big decision? How will you know, "Aha, now I have had enough of a break. Now it's time for me to come back and make a big decision." What will let you know?

Peggy: I need to talk to my mom.

Insoo: Talk to your mom, okay.

Peggy: I just need to talk to her, you know. I'm 35 years old, you'd think I wouldn't, but I just wanna talk to my mom.

Insoo: Yeah, sure.

Peggy: Then I'll figure it out. I'll figure it out then.

Insoo: So your mom has been very supportive, it sounds like.

Peggy: She doesn't know about Bob yet.

Insoo: Right, but when she finds out, you know she's going to be very supportive of you.

Peggy: Yeah, I've got really good parents.

Insoo: Yeah, good. You're very fortunate. Other people, are there other people in your life who would be that supportive of you?

Peggy: I've got friends.

Insoo: Friends. Uh-huh. Good friends?

Peggy: I have some good friends.

Other times, empathy is communicated nonverbally through the therapist's facial expression, soft tone of voice, or gentle look. I (YD) am reminded of a dog I once had who functioned as a sort of informal receptionist for me. My psychotherapy office was attached to our home. The dog would greet my clients at the front door and, without touching them, quietly escort them to my office. Only if my clients touched the dog would she nuzzle them to be petted. Unless my client requested that the dog stay during the session, I would ask her to "Go out, now." She always obeyed me and exited promptly.

Except once. A man I had seen for depression over the previous month had come into my office for his appointment. Things had been going well for him for the past two sessions and I imagined that this might be our last. However, when I walked into my office I noticed that my dog had placed her head on the man's knees and was quietly licking his hand. When I asked her to leave, she completely ignored me, kept her head on the man's lap, and gazed into his face.

I was so surprised by my dog's uncharacteristic behavior and the man's intense absorption with her gentle affection that, not knowing what to do and sensing that I should respect what was going on, I just sat silently. After a few moments, the man cleared his throat laboriously and explained in a shaky, infinitely sad voice, "My girlfriend was raped last night. I just found out. I feel so terrible, I could barely make it here. I don't know how your dog knows, but I swear she knew what I was feeling. That's why she wouldn't obey you." I believe he was right. My sweet dog stayed throughout the session and comforted the poor man with her head against his knees as he talked about his feelings of shock, hurt, and anger and gradually formulated a plan about what he could do to help himself and his girlfriend get through the next few days. At the end of the session, he repeated, "I don't know how your dog knew, but I swear she *knew* what I was feeling before I could even put it in words." All that empathy without a word between them!

Some people use words to convey empathy; others convey it nonverbally; still others convey it verbally but indirectly through what they say and the kinds of questions they ask as well as through what they don't say or ask. For example, if someone has just lost a loved one, an empathic friend would probably not ask for a time-consuming favor or burden the mourner with the friend's problems. Empathy is a complicated business. An expression of caring needs to be understood by the receiver and congruent with the communicator's personality style in order to be believable. It is context that makes it possible for the receiver to decode the message and make meaning out of it.

I have long suspected that empathy is one of those things that can be learned but not taught. I think the best way to learn it, apart from through life experience, is to listen intensely to our clients. They will tell us how it feels to be them through their tone of voice, facial expressions, and especially through the stories they tell about their lives.

Chapter 2

WHAT DREAMS MAY COME: STORIES OF MIRACLES AND SOLUTION BUILDING

In the introduction we mentioned the fairy tale *Rumpelstiltskin,* in which the protagonist accomplishes the seemingly impossible task of spinning straw into gold. SFBT therapists invite their clients to experience a type of psychological alchemy when they ask them the miracle question (see page 7). The magic of the miracle question is that it directs clients' attention to the immediate future—as soon as tomorrow morning—and then invites them to begin the virtual process of psychologically transforming the straw into gold. In responding to the miracle question, clients spontaneously begin generating their ideas of a problem-free state. Often these are thoughts clients have vaguely entertained in the past but never articulated. The miracle question empowers clients to reach into their previously untapped resources and begin the first small steps toward creating solutions that can transform "impossible dreams" into realities.

Telling and Listening
Contributed by John Sharry, Dublin, Ireland

In therapy sessions with more than one person, the miracle question often succeeds in bringing together the individuals seeking help, even when their answers to the miracle question differ slightly. This was the case with the family of seven-year-old Paul.

Paul came to the child and family clinic with his father and mother because he had been exhibiting extreme anxiety after witnessing a car accident that had occurred near his home five months earlier. In the first session, Paul's parents, Sue and Jim, told me that every time Paul heard a car skidding or speeding he became frightened and sometimes would "lose it and go ape." They found these outbursts upsetting. Paul also had nightmares and complained about pains in his head in the middle of the night. He often refused to spend the night at home, preferring to sleep at his grandparents' house. This had led to a lot of conflict: If his mother insisted that he stay at home, Paul would throw a tantrum or suffer a panic attack.

Paul spoke readily to me about his distress and how he was worried that cars were going to crash. He remembered the accident very clearly and could describe it. He explained that at night he sometimes awoke frightened because he thought "the devil" was after him. When I asked Paul how he coped with all this, he answered that he stayed at his grandmother Nanny's house a lot because there were no "skid cars" there. He explained that he slept better when he wasn't as worried.

At this point, Sue said she didn't like him staying at Nanny's and thought he should come home and live normally. People outside the family were telling her that she should insist that Paul stay home. Sue said she felt guilty because she didn't know how many of his fears were real and how many of them he was making up to get his own way. I reflected that it was clear Sue wanted to do the right thing for Paul, to help him live at home and not put him under pressure.

Paul's father described the difficulty he had dealing with Paul's panic attacks. When I asked him how he coped, Jim said he took Paul in his arms and soothed him until the panic went away. Jim worried that the attacks had gone on too long after the accident, and he agreed with his wife that Paul should return to living at home full-time. Both parents admitted that Paul "ruled the roost" at home and they found it hard to get him to do anything. They added that this had contributed to the conflict between them.

As the interview progressed, I learned of several exceptions to the problems with Paul's behavior and reactions. Both parents described how Paul was very good at school. He had just recently received a report from his teacher who described him as a "helpful, thoughtful boy." When I asked him how he had managed to get such a good report, Paul answered, "I just do what my teacher tells me, and she says I'm a good writer." I explored how Paul was able to "do just what she says," and learned that when he concentrated on his schoolwork, his mind never wandered and he was able to forget his fear.

Paul also spoke of the friends he had at school and talked about what they did together. He then talked about being at Nanny's house and how he felt safer there. I asked Paul what he did to feel safe there, and he explained that there were not many cars in the area. However, most of his friends lived near his home, and he missed them when he was with Nanny. I commented that it would be nice if he could feel safe and be with his friends. Jim and Sue said that prior to the accident Paul had been very different and played in the area near their house. Paul also remembered this and described how he was not afraid then—"I just looked at the skidding cars and I didn't mind."

When I asked them the miracle question, Sue said she wanted Paul to be less afraid and not run to the corner every time he heard a car. Instead, he would be calm and relaxed. She added that she also would handle Paul's panic better herself. When I asked how she would know she was handling the panic better, Sue said she would be calmer herself. Jim said he wanted Paul to be the way he was before the accident—"a happy-go-lucky child with plenty of friends." Paul said he wanted to get back to playing with his friends in the front yard and staying overnight at home because his mom and dad wanted him to. I summarized these goals, pointed out the great similarity between them, and commented that I thought they could work well together to achieve them.

I then asked the family to scale how close they were to achieving their goals. On a scale of 0 to 10, with 0 signifying no progress and 10 signifying that the problem was solved, Sue rated herself at a 0.5 and Jim rated himself at 1. Jim expressed doubt about making progress because they "had already tried everything." When I asked what had given him a little bit of hope (i.e., a 1 instead of a 0), Jim said that things were better now than they had been a few weeks ago, when Paul's nightmares were really bad. After a pause he said that he could see the problems "just easing away by themselves."

Sue said she worried Paul had something "wrong with him" because he was so anxious. The 0.5 was a sign of hope that maybe things would, in fact, just ease away. She said she would feel more confident as she became more sure that there was nothing majorly wrong. Paul was the most optimistic, saying he was at an 8. He explained that he could go out and play with his friends if he wanted to do so.

I used a variation of the SFBT intrasession break in which I invited the family to take a few minutes to talk among themselves about what had been discussed so far, evaluate the important points in the session, and decide which ideas they wanted to explore for the remainder of the session.*

When I asked what ideas they had come up with during the intrasession break, Sue said she wanted to be calmer when dealing with the panics, Jim said he could distract Paul by taking him out during the times when he was most likely to panic (6–8 P.M.), and Paul mentioned that he wanted to play soccer with his friends. Sue then asked me if I thought Paul would get over his fears. I said I agreed with Jim that the fears would probably "ease away" and that they were a normal response to what had happened, especially because Paul had so recently been a happy-go-lucky child, which meant he could be one again. The fact that Paul was such a considerate, thoughtful boy who was noticed by his teachers and others, that he helped so much in the session to think things out, and

---

*I give feedback and suggestions only to families that specifically request it because I find that quite often the family's own formulations and descriptions are sufficient to gain the changes they want.

that he had two such concerned parents meant that I could be very confident that they could achieve their goals and solve the problem. I then complimented Sue on her awareness of how her own behavior might affect Paul and on her bravery in deciding to change. I suggested to the family that they make note of any changes that occurred before the next appointment.

In the second session the family immediately reported that there had been a great improvement at home. Paul had stayed at home overnight and rejoined the soccer team, which he really enjoyed. When a van drove past the house while Paul was playing with friends in the yard, he didn't get frightened. In fact, he went inside to tell his mother proudly, "I didn't get scared." I was curious about how the change had occurred and explored this with the family. Sue said she thought talking to me had made the difference. "I was surprised at how much Paul said, and he said even more on the way home in the car. It made me think how important it is to listen to him." I asked if she had tried this out. She explained that "instead of overreacting when he got upset, I just sat down and listened to what he was saying and he sort of came through it—it was amazing. . . . I learned a lot from how you listened to him." Jim said he thought "Paul just solved it himself. I realized last week that he could do that." I asked Jim what he had seen in Paul that had made him realize this. Jim answered, "Well, he is very intelligent, the teacher is always giving him good reports. . . . When we came here last time I was really surprised at how he was able to speak out and say what he wanted and what he was thinking. I think he just came out of the panics himself." Paul had a third explanation: "I wanted to play with my friends. I promised Mum and Dad that I would stay at home forever and they promised to bring me to soccer." I pointed out that Paul had "kept a deal with Mum and Dad just like you do in school."

Though things weren't fully solved (Paul had a few more panic attacks and tantrums), the family decided that they were sufficiently "on track" and didn't need to come again. They left knowing they could contact me in the future if they needed to.

So what made the difference? Each person had a different reason for the cause of change. Sometimes children's opinions about what they want can get lost in family therapy, especially when it is the parents who are pressing for change. But not allowing children to formulate their own views and goals can result in the loss of their cooperation and a needless hindrance to the work. In this case, Paul was given the time and space to take a position. Though each family member's goals were slightly different, there was enough in common for them to work in collaboration.

Jim, Sue, and Paul each gave a different explanation for why the desired change had taken place. All of these explanations were equally valid and helpful for the family. In fact, you could argue that the richer the diversity of explanation, the more enduring the change is. Within "solution talk" such multiplicity of explanations builds cooperation. This is in direct contrast to "problem talk," where multiple explanations can be the "cause" of problems and can lead to conflict and defensiveness because each explanation pinpoints someone to blame. In the more creative atmosphere of "solution talk," it is possible to envision multiple answers and attribute "positive blame" to everyone.

This case nicely illustrates the attentive listening that characterizes the optimal application of SFBT. This attentiveness is not lost on the clients, as Sue's comment illustrates: "I learned a lot from how you listened to him. . . . It made me think how important it is to listen to him." But SFBT is, of course, more than just listening. Throughout the sessions Sharry listened carefully for exceptions, which he then skillfully emphasized and expanded through his questions.

It often appears that parents and a child, especially an adolescent, have radically different goals. For example, parents may want the teenager or child to be "respectful" of their wishes for a curfew and use more polite language around the house, while the teenager may want the parents to "get off my back" or "leave me alone." It is helpful for the practitioner to pursue further details of what each side wants, by asking questions like, "Suppose your son is 'respectful' of your need to know where he is, what would be different between the two of you?" Equally important is to ask the teenager, "Let's just suppose your parents 'get off your back.' How do you imagine things will change between you and your parents?" Thus, we will be pursuing the individual meanings behind such cliché words as "respectful" or "get off my back." When the practitioner is patient and persistent enough, clients discover that their underlying desire is for both parties to get along, live in peace, have dinner together, maybe even watch some TV together.

Coming Together: Using the Miracle Question with People Who Have Multiple Ego States
Contributed by Lance Taylor, Calgary, Canada

An obvious question is: "What if the client says that his or her different alters have different miracles?" In the rare situations where this has happened, I (YD) respond by saying, "Well, since this is a miracle after all, let's suppose that in this miracle all of your alters could comfortably agree. What would be the first sign that your alters agree and what do you suppose the miracle they all agree upon would look like?" I have rarely, however, found it necessary to adjust the miracle question in reference to alters. The following case story illustrates how the miracle question can be effective with a client who has multiple ego states.

Zoe was a 45-year-old woman who came to her first appointment with her husband of six years, Jonathan. I began the session by asking how the couple had decided to come to treatment and learned that they had been referred by Zoe's physician. Together they had decided to accept the doctor's advice and consult with someone experienced with dissociative identity disorder (DID) so that they wouldn't "have to feel like [they were] crazy." Zoe and her husband confided that they recently had experienced a lot of stress, including some financial setback, and that in times of such stress Zoe's alternate personalities "popped out."

They gave an extended history of Zoe's psychiatric hospitalizations and described violent past encounters between Zoe and Jonathan. Zoe's earlier life history included sexual and physical abuse by her father as well as physical abuse by her first husband.

Beginning early in the session, Zoe repeatedly exhibited sudden and dramatic changes in her appearance, posture, tone of voice, accent, and vocabulary. At these times she or Jonathan would interject the names of her alters. They told me that Zoe had as many as 60 alters, some with names and some without. Some were more powerful than others, and some new alters seemed to emerge for the first time during periods of stress. There appeared to be a natural tendency for Zoe and Jonathan to engage in animated conversation about each alter, its history, and what its particular contribution to the conversation would be. Occasionally, Zoe would shift into another alter and become quite angry about "too many questions."

Eventually, I asked Zoe the miracle question. Zoe responded in the following manner: She held both of her hands out in front of her, pointed her outstretched fingers toward each other, brought her hands together so that her fingers intertwined, and speaking in the German accent of one of her alters, answered, "fewer gaps and blanks." Signs that the miracle had happened when she got up in the morning included knowing what to eat and drink and knowing whom to talk to. I asked a scaling question and Zoe rated herself at a 2 on a scale from 0 to 10 in which 10 signified, in her words, "coming together." Jonathan said he thought she was a 3. When I asked Zoe to explain why she rated herself at a 2 rather than a 0, she said, "We have come here today and we are talking about solving the problem."

As we further discussed the problem, Zoe described "not being able to control the coming and going of the alters." However, I had noticed that partway through the first session Zoe had mentioned that she kept the alters inside when she was at work, "because they are not permitted there." Furthermore, it was also apparent that in the beginning of the discussion, at significant points in the session, and when the conversation resumed after an intrasession break, Zoe entered into the more "together" persona.

As the first session concluded, I complimented Zoe for being at a 2 or 3 on her scale of "coming together," and for having such a good goal of, in her words, "feeling like me, coming together, and getting rid of gaps and blanks, or at least making them smaller." I asked Zoe to watch for times that were more relaxed, as well as to pick out the times when she was more "together," and make a note of what she was doing differently.

At the start of the second session, I asked Zoe to describe what was better. She responded: "being away traveling by myself for four days last week, staying in bed as long as I wanted, not being afraid of upsetting Jonathan, going out for several walks during the day without having to explain why, not eating lunch on time, and not having someone to get upset about that." Toward the end of the second session, Zoe expressed pride in "how much less prominent the alters were today." I complimented her on the "coming together" this showed. Zoe asked Jonathan if he would refer to her more as Zoe so as not to "pull the strings of various alters." I noted this, and afterward I was careful to use the name that Jonathan and Zoe were using whenever "an alter was out." Throughout the course of treatment, I neither engaged in nor encouraged discussion about the unique identity of an alter, its history, or its relationship to other alters. Whenever possible, I reoriented the session toward Zoe's goals, emphasized the positive differences she had noticed, and invited her to speculate on the causes for those successes. The "coming out of alters" did not occur after the fifth session. As of the second session, Zoe had been able to give good examples of improvements that had occurred since she had last seen me. She was also more than willing to talk about these small differences in detail.

I saw Zoe for 14 sessions over a period of 11 months. The first few sessions included Jonathan. Between the fourth and fifth session the couple separated briefly and then permanently separated between the ninth and tenth sessions. After some angry exchanges they decided to divorce. Subsequently, Zoe set this goal for her therapy: She would stop therapy after she had lived six months on her own, had cried about the loss of her marriage, and was making her own choices about her personal life.

At the end of the 13th session, Zoe had managed to live on her own for five months, was supporting herself with her own job, and was beginning to explore a relationship with a new man. She took her medical alert bracelet to a jeweler to have DID removed, so that she would be "treated like a normal person." I encouraged her to "keep going and watch for further signs of going forward *with her own life in the direction [she chose]" after therapy ended. She was also invited to call the clinic at any time in the future if she needed to. Zoe did resume therapy approximately one year later for a brief series of sessions to further address relationship issues.*

Taylor's work with Zoe illustrates how focusing on solutions can accomplish much more than just resolving the problem of "pathological symptoms" like hearing voices. Zoe actually alters her sense of identity from a mentally ill person to someone who would be "treated like a normal person." This is a dramatic example of how problem definition is unrelated to solutions. If we substituted the symptoms of DID with a multitude of other symptoms that we are presented with every day, Zoe's sessions would resemble any other session.

This case is an excellent example of the disconnect between problems and the solutions to them. While being respectful of the client's perception of the nature of her problem, Taylor masterfully sidestepped the issue—the alters—and focused on the client's goal of "coming together," reducing the "gaps" in her memory, and feeling in control of her life. When Taylor noticed that Zoe was able to control the appearance of her alters at work, he used that ability to help Zoe proceed toward her goal. This skillful therapist knew what to listen for and what to ignore. Although Taylor recognized that the alters' appearance was reinforced, supported, and perhaps unwittingly encouraged by Jonathan (to the degree that conversation about her alters seemed to have become the glue that held the relationship together), he wisely kept this observation to himself and, again, proceeded with the client's goal.

The disappearance of symptoms like those of Zoe forces us to question whether such serious clinical symptoms are socially constructed and reinforced when those symptoms are focused upon. In Zoe's case, the therapist's refusal to support, reinforce, and repeatedly talk about the alters had something to do with their disappearance and possibly with the couple's decision to divorce. Taylor's suggestion about what to look for—that is, the signs that Zoe was "coming together"—is very typical of most SFBT sessions.

HOW DO YOU WORK WITH CLIENTS FOR WHOM THE MIRACLE INVOLVES GETTING SOMEONE ELSE TO CHANGE?

Don't be discouraged by clients who believe that the solution to their problems begins with someone else changing. Listen to the following dialogue in which a client who is frustrated with her husband thinks of ways of changing her own behavior. The beauty of these questions is that the clients generate the answers while the therapist encourages them to provide even more details of the solution.

> Client: The only way that I will know that the miracle happened is when my husband wakes up lying next to me, maybe even touching me. It's been like we are two strangers in the same bed. I'll know when he touches even just my hair, or is close enough to touch my arm, and if he doesn't take his hand away if he accidentally brushes against me. It will take a miracle for him to notice that I am even there.
>
> Therapist: Suppose he does notice you. . . . What would he say if he were to explain how you will be different the morning after the miracle?
>
> Client: Oh, then I will be nice to him. I will want to talk to him in a nice tone instead of yelling at him and accusing him of sleeping around. He makes me crazy with his not talking to me. He treats me like I'm not there.
>
> Therapist: What would he say you would do instead of yelling at him?
>
> Client: I will talk to him in a nice tone, like we are friends instead of enemies.

From this brief dialogue you can see that it does not matter who begins the positive cycle; as long as a new pattern of interaction is established, a solution-building process can begin. If the wife alone comes to see the therapist, it will be easier to get her to initiate changing the pattern by talking to her husband in a soft, gentle voice. If both husband and wife come, the husband probably will be very intrigued by his wife's idea about what the first step should be, and he may have his own ideas—based on their days of courtship or marriage—as well.

Violet: Dealing With "Impossible" Situations
Contributed by Tahira Iqbal, Oslo, Norway

Sometimes what appears to be the solution may be literally impossible to achieve. In these cases, no amount of change on the part of the client will affect the situation or other individuals' behavior. These circumstances can make clinicians experience feelings of confusion and helplessness similar to those of the client. It is natural to want to work harder and longer or bring on more resources when we are confused or feel helpless to relieve suffering. This is a natural reaction to impossible situations. But focusing on the problem from the same angle as the client is not going to produce a new perspective. This story about Violet, a Muslim woman living in a strictly religious and unique cultural environment, illustrates this point perfectly.

I work as a "natural helper," or indigenous healthcare worker, in the immigrant neighborhood of the Old City section of Oslo. Home to Vietnamese, Cambodians, Bosnians, Indians, Pakistanis, Iranians, Africans, and others of various ethnicities, this area has the highest population density in all of Norway. I work as an advocate for the community's Muslim women, who are extremely restricted in their movement and social contact. I spoke of Violet's dilemma at a seminar Insoo Kim Berg taught in Oslo recently.

Violet came to me because she was experiencing extreme pain all over her body, especially in her shoulders. With no energy, she looked close to dead. I learned that her family situation was very complicated and that she had no one except me to talk to.

Violet had been married for several years to a hot-tempered man who was very physically abusive to her. They had two children. One night after an argument, her husband suddenly divorced her. According to Muslim law, a husband can divorce his wife at any time simply by repeating the words "I divorce you" three times. The father usually assumes custody of the children because it is believed that the children belong to the father, but Violet's husband allowed the children to live with her.

Violet eventually married another man, who was a teacher with a good education. Unlike her first husband, this man was very kind and gentle and honored Violet with respect. She gradually began falling in love with her second husband. Then, Violet's first husband decided that he wanted to remarry her, and he began pressuring her family to have her returned to him.

Violet's family wanted her to return to her first husband. The relationship between his family and theirs had become strained because of the divorce, and her family felt that things between the two families would be made right again if Violet returned to him. Her second husband said that if Violet wanted to return to her first husband, he would give her a divorce because he loved her very much.

Violet's first husband also began threatening to take her children away from her, which meant that she would never see them again. Losing one's children is the most terrible thing that can happen to a Pakistani mother, and Violet told me she felt as if she were dying inside every time she thought about it. Furthermore, even if her first husband didn't take the children, if she and her second husband had children, her children from the first marriage would become a second-class caste. The thought of that was unbearable for her.

Violet was very confused about the situation and kept asking me what to do. Of course, I didn't know the answer either. "Do I have to cry for my children for the rest of my life?" she asked. I didn't know what to say. I looked for answers to Violet's dilemma both in the Koran and from Muslim tradition. The Koran is very clear about how a man must respect and honor his wife and children, but, unfortunately, people do not always practice what the Koran says. I kept asking myself, "How can I give her the courage she needs?"

After listening to my presentation of this case during the seminar, Insoo quietly asked me what might be the worst thing that could happen to Violet. I had never thought about this. I had been thinking about her pain, her dilemma, her confusion, and had been looking for a way to help her out of her confusion. Then Insoo *suggested that, for the time being, perhaps being confused was a good thing for Violet, because it prevented her from making a decision before she is ready to do so. Under the circumstances, it was perfectly normal for Violet to be confused. Her decision would influence many lives in addition to her own.*

When Insoo said this I felt as if a weight had been removed from my shoulders. That evening, after I put my children to bed, I visited Violet. I told her that I had been troubled by her situation and had spoken to a large group of Norwegian and American professionals about it. I explained how they had expressed respect for her courage and admiration for her strength in having gone through so much as a young woman.

Violet was very curious about this. She said she felt honored and asked me what the professionals had said about her situation. I told Violet that they said she had every reason to be confused, and that perhaps the confusion was even helping her by preventing her from making a hasty decision just to escape the pain of indecision. Violet visibly relaxed and cracked a faint smile. This was the first time I had ever seen her smile, even a little bit. I saw Violet again two days later. She told me that she was getting out of the apartment with her two children for the first time in a long time, and the pain in her shoulders was a little bit better. After almost a year of hard work for Violet and myself, after some touch and go, as of this writing she is still married to her second husband and the children are still living with her. There has been no further violence against her from her first husband. When I see Violet on the streets, she greets me with a broad smile.

Most of us have faced an extreme dilemma in which either choice is equally painful. Sometimes the most useful thing to do is to shift one's focus in order to create a new perspective and possibly a new solution. Suggesting that a client go slowly and not make a decision under pressure and confusion buys some time and increases the likelihood that a new perspective will emerge.

Insoo's comment that Violet's confusion could protect her from making a decision before she was ready reminds me (IKB) of the resources that sometimes characterize problems and the importance of respecting the uniqueness of each person's life situation. Sometimes, as in cases like Violet's, what initially looks like a characteristic of the problem may in fact be the best available solution.

When a client describes a problem that seems impossible to improve, I often ask, "Is there any advantage in things continuing the way they are? Because it may be important to preserve that advantage." I am always very careful to emphasize the potential value of preserving the advantage, because I believe there are unique resources contained within each person and the life situations he or she confronts. Sometimes the advantage of the continuance of a problem can be preserved even if some aspects of the problem change. Other times, like in Violet's situation, it is clearly not advantageous or helpful for immediate change to occur. I believed that Violet would know when and if it was appropriate for her confusion to lift. Honoring her confusion seemed to me a wise and compassionate approach to a very complex situation.

Breaking Off, Breaking Through: Focusing on Solutions Rather than Problems
Contributed by Daniel Mentha, Bern, Switzerland

SFBT is focused first on constructing goals for the client and second on developing "solutions," or the means and ways of reaching those goals. These solutions can be different behaviors and/or changed constructions of reality.

As well-known ethnomethodologist Gale Miller says, problems are the social glues that hold our lives together; they organize and give meaning to our lives (personal communication, 1999). Most clients arrive at our offices with only the knowledge of what pains, upsets, or depresses them, because this is what they have long been preoccupied with. Therefore, figuring out what the client wants *instead* of the problem is a difficult and sometimes painstaking process. However, once a client figures out what will replace the problem, therapy seems to move rather rapidly. Notice how Daniel Mentha helps the client in this story to shift her focus from her problems to the real-life ways of solving them.

I routinely send a follow-up form to all my clients between 6 and 12 months after their last session. Some choose to answer, some don't. Recently a former client surprised me. Anna had dropped out of treatment but reported on the form that she had reached her goals. I decided to ask for a follow-up interview.

In our first session, 21-year-old Anna had described her life as a disaster. She had quit school twice, although she knew that both schools were within her intellectual ability. She couldn't decide what to do with her life, so she left home, moved to another city, and began an apprenticeship in a store as a clerk. The apprenticeship was unbearable to her. She ran into problems with customers and with her boss all day long, day after day. She was now seriously considering quitting. She vacillated between feeling despairing and feeling extremely energetic, almost to the point of hyperactivity or even euphoria. But most of the time she reported that she was feeling "pissed off" at work. She hated her apartment and visited her parents' home as often as possible in order to avoid the loneliness that forced her to face her sense of failure.

In our first session we looked for goals and exceptions. Anna wanted to get rid of her miserable feelings. She wanted to feel energetic and self-confident. She knew she had to do something about her professional impasse. But she said that before anything else, she wanted to "take herself seriously," "listen to herself," and go her "own way." On a goal attainment scale, Anna saw herself at a 0.5.

We discovered some exceptions but Anna thought they were a fluke because she could not explain how she managed to feel better on certain days. She had no ideas about how to provoke more good days or about how to make periods of good days last longer. It seemed, however, that she had a bit more control over feeling good when she was occupied with her hobbies instead of working.

During the break I decided not to give her a task. Although there were exceptions, Anna had no idea how she brought about those times when she felt a little bit better. I decided, therefore, that asking her to recreate those days could lead to a further sense of failure, and instead I validated her sense of despair and confusion. I told her that I agreed with her goals of "listening to herself," "following her own way," and doing things to "please herself." I speculated that perhaps life had taught her more about others' expectations of her than it had taught her about her own expectations of herself. I added that she already seemed to know what pleased her about her hobbies and leisure activities, and I complimented her on understanding what she didn't want, telling her it was "a first and important step."

In the second session I asked the miracle question. Anna answered that after the miracle she would have different feelings in her body. She would live in a different environment, in nature, and there would be new people. Her sister would notice that she was more open instead of angry. They both would want to spend more time together talking, cooking, and maybe planning a holiday. Her mother would see her as more vivid, energetic, ambitious, and purposeful. At first her mother would not react enthusiastically. She would need time to be convinced that the change was real, but eventually she would feel less of a need to question Anna, which would be a relief for Anna. They would be able to talk together again. Anna's father also would notice the changes and react like his wife. He would want to see Anna acting on her own initiative. Anna predicted that her relationship to both parents would become more distant for a time immediately following the miracle.

At that point it was clear that Anna not only wanted to live up to her own expectations, but also wanted to become trustworthy in her parents' eyes again. Her goal now was to find a place to live and a new job where she could feel good. On the goal attainment scale, Anna saw herself at a 7. When I asked her to describe the difference between her previous 0.5 and the current 7, Anna explained that her consciousness had changed. She now realized that she had to exert herself much more. She could identify the details of her next small steps: talking more frequently and differently to customers and superiors and to her parents and sister. In my feedback after the break I pointed out that her being at a 7 showed that she had the means to markedly and rapidly improve her situation. Now she needed to find a way to continue this short-term change.

When Anna did not show up for her next session, I suspected that she had "relapsed." I sent her a letter in which I invited her to decide whether she wanted additional sessions. She telephoned me and scheduled another appointment but again did not show up. I sent a second letter with more or less the same content as the first, but she didn't answer it.

When she returned her follow-up form 17 months later, she remembered being at a 7 in our final session and said she was now at a 9. She wrote that she had completely regained her self-confidence and that she could handle stress much better. She had also improved her capacity to find and execute solutions, although there was still more room for improvement. She was confident she could improve this on her own. She no longer fell into "depressionlike states," and handled her everyday life satisfactorily. She felt "completely independent." Although her current job was stressful and demanding, she was not having difficulty with conflicts and her depression had not reappeared. She perceived working as "a necessary means to an end."

In our follow-up interview, she explained that in looking back at 17 months ago, she realized for the first time that all the changes had to come from herself, rather than expecting things to just happen. Answering the "magic question" (miracle question) in the second session made her realize that everything had to start from herself, and blaming her family or her boss was not helpful or useful and it was not their job to make it happen for her! I asked whether in our second session she had seen her positive development and confidence. She replied that she had not been very confident at that time, but the confidence and motivation to stay on track had increased with time and with success. She had received no further professional help, but talking to family members and peers had helped her stay on track. She now felt very confident and motivated to continue moving forward.

It seems that Anna had some difficulty figuring out what she wanted to put *into,* rather than take out of, her life. Of course, Anna was wise enough to know that filling her life with something positive would not happen in the therapy room—it would happen by living life. By visualizing solutions rather than problems, Anna grew up and realized that only she could take the steps to change her life.

Chapter 3

SORTING THE WHEAT FROM
THE CHAFF: FINDING EXCEPTIONS

SFBT assumes that there are exceptions to all problems—that all clients' lives contain successes, however small and infrequent. Exceptions are those situations, times, events, or episodes when the usual problem could have occurred but somehow didn't. The therapeutic task is to examine those exceptions and get the client to repeat the successful mastery of the problems. For example, a child who has terrible behavior problems at home may not be so difficult to manage in school, at friends' houses, or with Grandma or Grandpa. A child who misbehaves in school may not have problems with all teachers; he might behave well in art class or gym even though his science teacher describes him as "hell on wheels."

The assumption that there are exceptions to problems gives clients hope and challenges common statements like, "He never gets along with anyone." Rather than pointing out that using words like "never," "always," or "all the time" is not factual and thus not allowed, SFBT therapists gently ask parents or school personnel, "Tell me about the times when Jimmy seems to get along with others, even for a short time." This is a more respectful way to remind the teachers, parents, or other adults around the child that there are times, however brief or infrequent, when Jimmy does behave.

There are situations when clients say that there are no exceptions: "I've felt depressed all my life, it seems," "I am so tired of being tired," or they describe a chronic state of feeling defeated or hopeless. The temptation to agree with the client is great in these situations; however, your feeling hopeless about the client will only add to the client's hopelessness. Therefore, you may need to take a different tack, by using a "coping question." Some examples of coping questions are:

- It seems like you have been depressed for a long time and it is really amazing that you have hung in there all this time. What keeps you going under such difficult circumstances?
- Wow, you've been through a lot! How do you manage such difficult situations everyday?
- Most people in your situation would have given up on your child a long time ago. What helps you to hang in there?
- How do you explain to yourself that you are doing as well as you are doing under such difficult circumstances?
- What a remarkable person you are! Where did you learn to be so loving in spite of the fact that you did not have a good role model as a child?

You can imagine how clients might respond to your genuine admiration for their strength and refusal to give up on themselves. Even their decision to talk to you is a sign of hope. Such resources and determination must be pointed out and looked at carefully. Most clients are startled by this fresh view of their life; they perk up and begin to describe their faith, values, religious beliefs, or various influences that made them strong and persistent. It is a good idea to follow up on these responses, maintaining your initial curiosity and admiration.

A Very Optimistic Man:
Working With Clients With Acute Chronic Pain
Contributed by Kotaro Fujioka, M.D., Shizuoka, Japan

The following case is an excellent example of how a compassionate physician's skillful use of coping questions can make a difference in working with a client in a seemingly hopeless situation.

This story about a man with chronic, excruciating pain shows just how miraculous the discovery of an exception can ultimately be.

I am a medical doctor and I was working with 67-year-old Mr. Tanaka, who was admitted to the hospital where I consulted. He had attempted suicide with an overdose of sleeping pills. Mr. Tanaka had been tortured by severe pain for 50 years as a result of the tubercular meningitis he contracted when he was 15 years old. His case was exceptional both in terms of the severity of his pain and the extreme length of his suffering—chronic pain is not common in Japan, and many doctors dislike chronic pain cases because they are troublesome to treat.

A recurring tubercular infection of the spine had caused Mr. Tanaka to suffer burning and intolerable pain, and he had endured over 30 sequesterotomy operations to remove infected bone. His spine was bent like the letter S, and with each operation his pain had become worse. Eventually these operations totally destroyed his spine below the chest, causing burning and stabbing pain in his lower limbs, and he had to use a wheelchair. His repeated attempts to get relief from the medical community had proven unsuccessful, and his case had eventually been abandoned.

Despite his handicap, Mr. Tanaka had managed to become a successful commercial designer and was known to be a hard worker. At the time of his suicide attempt, however, he was retired. Unable to control his pain even a little, he stayed home suffering all day and eventually lost all hope. This had led to his suicide attempt.

I treated Mr. Tanaka in the hospital after the suicide attempt, and I was not hopeful about the possibility of medical treatment because previous treatment had been less than exceptional. We tried all the available physical therapies, nerve-block therapies, and drug therapies, but unfortunately we found them all ineffective. Only morphine was marginally effective, relieving about 40 percent of his pain, and even this did not last. Raising the dose did not help, and before long the man's pain and disability returned to the same excruciating level he had suffered before.

I had hesitated to use psychotherapy up to this point, thinking that Mr. Tanaka's pain clearly originated in his badly damaged body and that a psychological approach would not relieve his agony. However, having exhausted all the options, I decided to try the

SFBT that I was learning at the time. In order to do this I had to pretend to believe that the man really did have the necessary psychological resources.

When I visited him at home (where he was receiving nursing care because of a severe bed sore), we had the following conversation:

> Doctor: I have been quite curious about you. How have you gotten through your painful life without giving up on everything?
> Mr. Tanaka: Well . . . because I am a very optimistic man. It helped me!
> Doctor: Oh! How is it helpful being an optimistic man?
> Mr. Tanaka: While the pain was awful, I worked very hard. It made me forget it even a little bit. I believed that the pain would be relieved someday.

At the end of the conversation, I told him: "When you feel even a little bit more comfortable, please remember that occasion and notice why and how it occurs."

Over the next few weeks, I repeatedly encouraged Mr. Tanaka to continue to notice exceptions to the pain. Six weeks later, he smiled and told me, "Since you began asking me about the times when I feel better, I have been considering it. A couple of days ago, on the way from the dentist, I stopped in the park at the riverside. I ate sandwiches there and gave crumbs to the pigeons. They started going after the crumbs, and I really enjoyed watching them. While I was watching them, I did not have any pain at all!"

Needless to say, I gave him the highest compliments on this. Later he reported that the time without pain was increasing. He started gardening and fishing at the park, and he took a short trip with his wife. The improvements in his condition still continue seven years later, and recently he began to go to the daycare center for physical training.

Changing a Pachinko Habit:
Working with an Addict Who Doesn't Seem Motivated
Contributed by Kikuko Isogai, Fukuoka, Japan

Even in cases where clients initially appear unmotivated to change their addictive behavior, there are always exceptions. That they have shown up for therapy at all suggests that they want something, if only to get the person who referred them (often a spouse or a probation officer) off their back. In this story, the client's past history suggested he was highly unmotivated to give up his gambling, despite disastrous financial consequences. However, by focusing on the initially very small exceptions, the client began to grow more motivated until he was able to free himself from his behavior.

One week after New Year's Day, Ayn and Yoichi, a couple in their forties, came to our clinic. They had a 12-year-old son and a 17-year-old daughter. According to Ayn, Yoichi had become so obsessed with pachinko* that he had begun falling into debt repeatedly. So far, the debt had accumulated to about $210,000. Ayn had confronted her husband about the debt several times, and each time he vowed not to fall into debt again. The couple paid off the debt with the help of Yoichi's parents.

In spite of Yoichi's stable job, Ayn could no longer afford to buy herself clothes because of his debt. About three months before they visited the clinic, Yoichi had become involved with pachinko again. This time he left home and was missing for several weeks. He finally said he would come home on New Year's Eve, on the condition that his debts be paid off by his parents. The following dialogue took place when I met with the couple.

> *Therapist: What kinds of things would you like to discuss so that you will feel glad that you came in today?*
> *Ayn: Needless to say, I would like to talk about my husband's pachinko habit. But most of all, I just want him to come home.*
> *Yoichi: (Sullenly) I only came here because my wife asked me to. I can't stop playing pachinko because I am addicted. After work, I go straight to a pachinko parlor.*

---

*Pachinko is a game similar to slot machines and is one of the most popular forms of gambling in Japan. It is regarded as a very acceptable form of entertainment for people over the age of 18. Only recently it has been noted that pachinko is addictive and therefore creates social problems. For example, a mother engaged in playing pachinko left her child to die in an overheated car, and a housewife who fell into debt because of her addiction to pachinko ended up in prostitution.

Once I start to play I get so wrapped up that I just can't think of anything else. Not even about my family. If I return home I know my wife won't let me play pachinko. That's why I don't want to go home.

As the session progressed I eventually found out that Yoichi had not played pachinko for an entire week since New Year's Day.

Therapist: *How have you been able to stay away from pachinko for a whole week?*

Yoichi: *I haven't had the money to go because I am in too much debt.*

Therapist: *In the past you kept on borrowing money regardless of your debts. So how do you put up with not being able to go? I also think it is amazing that you have been able to keep your job while being so obsessed with pachinko. How did you do that?*

Yoichi: *I think I would be less than human if I kept betraying my family, my parents, and my friends any more than I already have.*

Ayn: (With tears in her eyes) *My husband is a good man and a good father if he does not play pachinko. Our daughter told me that she would drop out of high school and work so that her father could pay off his debts and come home every night. Our son also cares about his father.*

Therapist: (To Yoichi) *What would be helpful in order for you to continue to stay away from pachinko?*

Yoichi: *Once I start playing, I know I can't control myself. Whether I win or lose, it's hard for me to stop. So I think I had better quit altogether and find another hobby such as playing baseball or golf.*

Therapist: (To Ayn) *What do you think would be helpful in order for your husband to feel that he wants to go home every night?*

Ayn: *I would try to make our home comfortable for my husband. For instance, I would fix a nice meal or prepare a hot bath for him every night. I will also keep the house very clean. Since my husband likes to go out, we can go out for dinner or take a trip somewhere. I will try not to mention pachinko, particularly in the morning when he leaves for work.*

  The couple seemed to be approaching their solution. I attempted to elicit further information about the solution by asking the miracle question.

> Yoichi: *I would go home straight from work and clean the house before my wife gets home from her part-time job. Then we would eat dinner and watch television with our children. I might have a few beers and go to bed. I would go out with my friends from time to time. On weekends, I might get involved with my son's soccer team or play golf. The whole family might go to karaoke or play some outdoor sports.*
>
> Therapist: *How do you think your family would be different in response to this?*
>
> Yoichi: *My family is fine just as they have been. I just want them to go out with me on weekends. My family and I will have a lot more conversation since I have nothing to feel guilty about.*
>
> Ayn: (Agreeing with her husband) *We would chat with each other more while watching television. I think it is a good idea to go to an athletic field with our children.*

  At the end of the session, I told the couple that I appreciated their coming in spite of how hard it must have been for them. I acknowledged Ayn's willingness to support her husband in any way she could, as well as their children's concern. I also complimented Yoichi on his intention to quit pachinko and replace it with other activities for the sake of his family. Since the miracle question generated many good ideas of what the family would do when Yoichi is not playing pachinko, I suggested that they start with whatever seemed to be the easiest, simplest, and least expensive to do. Ayn said that she would call for another appointment if necessary.

  Approximately a year after the first session, Ayn made another appointment. With a resigned look on her face, she described the situation: "My husband began playing pachinko again and he hasn't come home for a whole month. My children and I went out looking for him every night. He finally came home again on New Year's Eve with huge debts." Yoichi sat next to his wife and kept his head down. I complimented Ayn on the loving concern she and her children had shown for their husband and father. Then I turned to him and decided to focus on his successful 11 months rather than his relapse.

> Therapist: *How were you able to manage so successfully for the 11 months before your relapse?*
> Yoichi: (Looking depressed) *I kept myself busy by managing my son's soccer team. But at the end of November when the soccer season was over . . . I don't know how it happened. I kept telling myself to stay away from pachinko and I was confident that I could.*

I acknowledged Yoichi's remorse and asked him what kinds of things he did to abstain from pachinko for 11 months. He explained that he went to work every day, went out for a drink with his friends at times, and took his parents and family on short trips. I asked the couple if Yoichi had ever quit pachinko for 11 months in the past and they both answered, "No, it was the first time in 20 years."

Ayn described what it had been like after Yoichi quit pachinko.

> Ayn: *He came home straight from work and cleaned the house. Our family spent some time together in the evenings. We lived peacefully for the first time in our married life.*
> Therapist: (To Yoichi) *Given those things that you were doing before your relapse, what would be helpful for you to start doing again so that your family life could become peaceful once more?*
> Yoichi: *My wife. She can help me to relax and spend time with my children.*
> Ayn: *He should be firm in his decision to quit, but I have to tell you that I could become more thoughtful of him,*

*too. I started to take things for granted when they were
going well. I realize that it's no use holding onto the
past, and I want all of us to move on.*

Then I asked Yoichi a scaling question regarding how motivated
he was to resume his stable life, with 0 being no motivation and
10 being maximum motivation.

Yoichi: *I'm about a 5. I'm not so sure if I can quit
pachinko right away.*
Therapist: *Okay, what would help you to move up 1 point
on the scale?*
Yoichi: *Soccer management meetings begin in two weeks.
Once they start I think I will be a 10.*

As feedback at the end of the session I commented on how dis-
appointing it was for everyone in the family that Yoichi had relapsed. "However," I said, "your family got along for the 11
months of his abstinence. It was the outcome of all your efforts
and it is wonderful. Since Yoichi has the prospect of quitting
pachinko once the soccer season begins, I suggest that you all do
more of the same things that you did for those 11 months."

As the couple walked out of the room, Yoichi said, "I'm glad
that I came today. I honestly thought that I could never quit
pachinko and that it would be no use coming here. But I think I
will give it one more try."

Three months later, Yoichi reported that he had been going home
directly after work, was talking with his family a lot, and had taken
his parents and family to a hot springs resort. In a follow-up conversation one year later, I learned that Yoichi had maintained his
abstinence during the soccer team's off-season and was confident
that he would be able to continue to manage his life without
pachinko.

Isogai respectfully and tenaciously continued to focus on exceptions throughout the sessions, even in the face of a very destructive problem. In doing this she gave the client room to restore

and retain his sense of self-respect and dignity as he gradually overcame his gambling habit and regained control of his life. Throughout the therapy, Isogai maintained a graceful balance of gentleness and respect, while never losing her focus on solution development.

One Word at a Time: Utilization in SFBT
Contributed by Karl Butinga, Hengelo, The Netherlands

In Ericksonian hypnotic utilization, the client's perceptions, strongly held beliefs, and behaviors were originally used both to ratify and strengthen hypnotic responses during a session and to strengthen the client's ability to respond to therapeutic posthypnotic suggestions following the session. Therapeutic utilization is the process of incorporating the client's ongoing perceptions and behaviors into the therapeutic change process. This case nicely illustrates how Erickson's concept of utilization has been given broader, nonhypnotic therapeutic applications in SFBT.

Inviting the client to identify and expand upon exceptions—and using the miracle question to prompt clients to use their perceptions, ideas, and values to imagine behaviors that would characterize their own unique solution—are ways of directly utilizing and incorporating the client's ongoing behaviors. Furthermore, the client's imaginary miracle behaviors are further utilized as the client enacts and further refines them to achieve the solution.

It was Christmastime and Marco was in first grade. Since kindergarten, he had been getting along well with his fellow students, and he was doing satisfactorily in all his school subjects—except spelling and reading. The teacher decided to make a special effort to help Marco, so for the remainder of the school year she privately tutored Marco while the other children were enjoying recess or breaks.

Unfortunately, this did not alleviate his spelling and reading problems, and when Marco started second grade the next year, a special remedial teacher was brought in to help him. Marco's parents also began to work with him after school during his free time at home each night and on holidays. This caused him to miss his playtime and the family activities he had enjoyed before his reading problems began. He started hiding his reading book from his parents at night, and his parents began punishing him for it.

By third grade, Marco was reading a little better than before, but not well enough to keep up with his class. He began stealing money from his mother and giving presents to his schoolmates. During that year's school vacation, his parents sat inside the house and read with him while the other children in the neighborhood played outdoors.

By fourth grade, Marco's younger sister had surpassed him in reading ability while he still struggled. Marco set a fire at school, and consequently was sent away from home to a residential institution, where I taught and served as director. I made the assessment that forcing Marco to read had only done harm and I decided to try a different approach. I told him in a friendly manner, "You can do what you want, but I advise you not to read until you are ready to read."

Because my family lived with me on the institution grounds and my son was the same age as Marco, it was natural that the two boys became friends. Marco began to come over to our house to play with my son. I was in the habit of affectionately scratching my son's back as I sat with him and read stories aloud in the evenings. This was something my son especially enjoyed.

Marco visited often and liked to sit with my son as they listened to the stories. As the weeks went by Marco became such a part of the family that it was natural for me to give him an occasional affectionate back scratch just as I did with my son during storytime. Marco obviously enjoyed this.

One evening after reading several stories, I said to Marco, "You enjoy stories, don't you?" Marco nodded. I told him, "I would like to help you learn to read more, and I think you can do more than you think you can. Will you allow me to do this?" Marco agreed, so I asked him, "Here (at home) or in my office?" Marco preferred the office. So we agreed to meet at 9 A.M. the next day.

The next morning in the office, I told Marco again, "I think you can do more than you think you can. Do you have an idea how you can solve the problem of reading?"

Marco answered, *"Just reading words."*
I asked permission, *"May I start?"*
Marco said, *"Yes."*
With a typewriter, I made a column of words. I typed a series of simple words to make up a sentence, but placed them vertically so Marco could look at just one word at a time. Reading one word at a time, Marco successfully read the words. Together they spelled out the message,

> See
> these
> words
> you
> already
> know.

I praised Marco enthusiastically for reading the words. At first Marco seemed happy with the praise, but then he looked troubled. After a few moments, he confided, *"When the words are on a page, I get confused."*

Using the same friendly, comfortable manner I had used in the past during storytime, I asked, *"May I give you some advice? Many children benefit if they just see one word at a time. You can use the edge of a piece of paper to block out the other words."* I told the other teachers to *"just praise Marco. Don't try to control him or challenge him."* Marco was able to solve his reading problem and return home within three months, and there were no further problems.

Marco eventually went on to complete a university education that required extensive reading skills. Now a grown man with a child of his own and a successful career, he recently paid me a visit to thank me for the help I gave him so long ago.

Butinga's first brilliant move was to invite Marco to enjoy the pleasure of reading instead of forcing him to learn. Being an experienced teacher, he recognized that Marco's desire to learn was the most important element in education. He found a way to blend this with Marco's desire to be accepted.

Butinga's intervention reflects the following SFBT principles:

- The client is respected and consulted as a competent expert on the problem and how to solve it (e.g., "Do you have an idea how you can solve your difficulty with reading?").
- Exceptions to the problem are identified and utilized through exploration and discussion. Additional exceptions are sought out until a solution is reached. For example, Marco usually felt distressed during reading experiences, but when the teacher read him stories and scratched his back, he relaxed and enjoyed himself. This allowed him to respond favorably to the teacher's offer to help.

Marco's response to the first solution-focused question ("just reading words") is utilized as a potential exception. It is expanded by incorporating another exception: the words he already knows from previous partial successes in school. By building upon these exceptions, Marco succeeds in reading vertically arranged words. Further expansion leads the teacher to suggest that Marco use a piece of paper to limit his focus to one word at a time. By building upon and expanding the exceptions, Marco can now read books.

Solution Bank:
Using SFBT in Group or Community Settings
Contributed by Keizo Hasegawa, Nagoiga, Japan

Having done more than 3,000 hours of group therapy, I (YD) have found that the miracle question and scaling questions translate especially well in group settings. When using the miracle question, I like to ask the person to speculate about how the other group members will notice that the miracle has happened. Then the other group members compliment the individual when they observe him or her exhibiting or describing new instances of the miracle behaviors described in the answer. Scaling can be used in a similar way in a group setting, with people being invited to guess where other members would rate themselves on a scale of achieving their ongoing goals. This prompts group members to notice the exceptions and positive behaviors that the person exhibits or describes from week to week.

Consistently using the miracle question and scaling in group settings encourages everyone in the group to validate each other's exceptions and miracle behaviors in addition to noting and appreciating their own. These groups become a very inspiring experience for everyone.

This story is a great example of how SFBT can be applied in a community setting to elicit exceptions to a very serious social problem.

In July of 1997, I was a member of a group that carried out a relatively extensive social psychological experiment using SFBT. The experiment took place at the highly regarded NHK, Fukushima's largest television broadcasting station, just south of Japan's seventh-largest city, Sendai.

The suicide of a boy named Okawauchi received a great deal of media attention in Japan in the '90s. A clever and considerate boy in his second year of middle school, he had been severely bullied by other students. His father had complained to the bully's parents prior to the boy's suicide, but they responded with indifference: "Adults shouldn't put their noses into children's business."

Okawauchi's mother, no longer able to tolerate seeing her son in such a desperate state, consulted the teacher, who separated the children. Eventually, however, the teacher put Okawauchi back in the group of bullies, hoping they would become friends. Left with no way out, Okawauchi took his own life, leaving behind a suicide note. Media coverage of Okawauchi's suicide prompted other children in similar situations to imitate him.

It was during one of these periods of youth suicides that we carried out the experiment with the television station. To raise public awareness of the problem, we had planned a special program called Bullying. *It was to be broadcast during peak viewing time. Our plan was to not only present opposing viewpoints and explore the dynamics of the current issue, but to also create a chain reaction of solutions to the problem.*

Advance publicity was posted two weeks prior to the program date so that we could solicit various solutions: "Please inform us of cases in which bullying issues were solved." Telephone banks were installed and we were ready.

Naturally, we were anxious—what if only problem cases were reported? This could exacerbate rather than remedy the problem.

To our relief, 10% of the callers reported bullying cases that had been resolved. Some solutions were simple—"When the teacher didn't respond to my complaints about the bullying, I talked to the principal, and the result was very positive"—while others were more sophisticated—"The teacher brought up the bullying issue at a class meeting and the children came up with solutions."

The television station was very pleased with the outcome of the program and it was seen as an innovative way to report on hot topics. More important, other local television stations asked us to put on similar programs for them. Subsequently, newspapers and radio stations have been more willing to publicize successful solutions not only on bullying, but also on other serious social problems, such as truancy, delinquency, and even family violence. The outcome of this experiment is called "Solution Bank," a Web site where students and parents can find out what others have done to solve the bullying problem. We are very proud of our effort to apply SFBT principles to large social problems.

This case illustrates the innovative and creative ways the SFBT approach can be adapted to address serious social problems. Here, the media was used to mobilize the community, and the community responded to the benefit of all the children.

Indira's Choices: The Art of Asking Questions
Contributed by Yvonne Dolan, Denver, Colorado

The questions we ask shape the answers our clients give us. Questions are the key to helping clients begin to change the story; they can subtly shift the way the story unfolds, like a gentle, soothing breeze that one hardly notices. A few well-phrased questions can express our assumption of client competence. For example, "Tell me about the time when you felt . . ." expresses a different assumption than "Have you had a time when you felt . . . ?" This story illustrates how the art of questioning can help clients gain confidence in themselves and uncover exceptions, even from long ago.

I cannot disclose the Western country in which this case took place because it could endanger the client. If her identity and history were revealed, she would be treated as an outcast by her entire family and ethnic community. There would also be some risk of physical harm.

Indira was a slim, attractive, well-dressed Arabic woman with a shy smile. Despite tastefully applied make-up and elegant jewelry, she looked much younger than her 20 years. When we were introduced, Indira spoke softly and articulately, often lowering her eyes. Her body was motionless, except for her hands, which moved constantly. I noticed her nails had been bitten.

Indira had immigrated with her parents when she was a young child. She and her parents, siblings, extended family, and friends were part of a self-contained community of families of similar ethnic and social background. She had never had a boyfriend and except for attending university courses, she never was allowed outside her home without a chaperon.

Unbeknownst to her family, Indira had been seeing a social worker at a mental health center for three years. She secretly broke the rules of her household by taking several buses to make her way from the school to the mental health center every few weeks.

The social worker had asked me for a consultation because even after three years of treatment, Indira continued to cut her arms regularly with a razor blade. The social worker had made many different suggestions, including having Indira write her feelings in a journal before cutting, substituting the cutting with making marks, and trying to make progressively smaller cuts. However, while Indira expressed a desire to stop the cutting, she always gave in to the urge to cut and failed to try the social worker's alternatives.

After exchanging greetings, Indira quickly explained that since the consultation had been scheduled, a new and very disturbing (though not totally unexpected) problem had arisen. She was clearly distraught. The day before our meeting, her parents had received an offer of marriage for her from the family of a respectable and accomplished young man. While born and raised in Indira's native village, the young man was currently completing his graduate studies at a large Western university far from his homeland.

I asked Indira what would need to happen in this session in order for it to be worthwhile for her. Indira explained that while the cutting was a concern for her, the marriage proposal was far more pressing. It would be necessary to give an answer in the next few days or risk insulting the boy's family. She knew she must make a decision, but she felt she couldn't bear any of the options. She didn't want to die, but she felt that suicide was the only way she could escape her impossible situation.

She explained her dilemma to us:

"I know this sounds simple to you, but it's not. Things are very different in my culture. You probably think I could just leave my parents' house, finish my university degree, and live on my own away from my relatives and friends. But if that's what you think you do not understand. My family means everything to me. If I lost my family and friends in our [expatriate] community, my life would be over. I would have no life. I would want to die. Even thinking about being rejected by them, I want to die. My whole life I have looked forward to this moment when a marriage proposal is offered.

"My parents are so happy. He is from a very nice family. And it is my chance, my only chance in our community for me to have a life of my own—my own house, my own husband and children, independence, and some freedom from my parents. In a way, I do not want to disappoint my parents by refusing the proposal. But I also don't want to give up the career I was hoping to have in medicine. My grades have been good, and if I go along with my parents, accept the proposal, and give up my studies, I will feel like my life is over. I may as well die. In fact, I would want to die. On the other hand, if I don't accept this proposal, I will either not get another one, or not get a very good one as a result of rejecting such a good family. In either case, I may never marry and have my own husband and children and household. This too, would mean to me that my life was over. In both cases it would feel intolerable. I think I would kill myself. And if I tell my parents, they will go crazy. They will kick me out of the house."

Indira began to weep softly as she explained what would happen if she accepted or rejected the proposal. Here is a portion of our conversation:

> Therapist: *I know this is very, very hard for you. You are having to make a very difficult decision.*

Indira: Yes, and neither decision feels right. They both feel hopeless.

Therapist: Is this the first difficult decision you have ever faced, or have there been other difficult ones you had to resolve in the past?

Indira: (She hesitates and looks questioningly at the social worker, who nods reassuringly.) *I guess the hardest decision I ever had to make was when my father's friend was molesting me. Since our families were close friends, I was frequently left at their house and I had no way to protect myself. It was kind of like this, only in some ways worse because I was really scared. But it was like this because either decision seemed impossible and it seemed at first that killing myself was the only option.*

The social worker explained at this point that the usual recourse of reporting the abuse to the police would have carried serious risk for Indira. If it was known in her family and her community that she had been raped, she would be considered unmarriageable, a disgrace to her family, and an outcast in her community. At best, she would live the life of a spinster aunt, staying as an unwanted guest in the home of one of her siblings, where she would be expected to be subservient and do housework and childcare. Furthermore, Indira was convinced that if she had told her father, he would have killed his friend, bringing terrible disgrace to both families and hurting many innocent people.

Despite these risks, two and a half years earlier Indira had bravely confronted her abuser alone and convinced him that if he ever tried to touch her again she would tell the police and everyone in her community. After that, the man avoided her and even seemed afraid of her. She had extracted a promise from him that he would never bother her again and that he would not attend her wedding or her college graduation even though her parents would naturally invite him.

I complimented both Indira and the social worker on doing such a good job handling the difficult and potentially dangerous situation. The social worker replied (indicating Indira), "She did it. I just gave her support." Indira looked at the social worker with tears in her eyes and said, "I couldn't have done it without you. I *was so alone. I would have killed myself if I hadn't come to you. You really helped me."*

I asked Indira how she had found the courage to seek out the social worker and ultimately to confront her abuser.

> Indira: Well, I had to talk to someone. One of my friends at school told me about this center. She had seen a social worker here and it really helped, so I made up my mind to go even though it meant breaking my parent's rules. I had to do it. With the abuse, I knew I had to do something because I just couldn't go on letting him do that.
>
> One of the things that really got to me, that I really couldn't stand as I got older, was the thought that someday he would be attending my wedding, sitting right up there with my family as if nothing had ever happened. I wanted to make him promise that he would make some excuse for not attending my wedding. It made me so angry. I just decided, he's not going to get away with this. I made up my mind. And when I confronted him, he actually looked scared. I know I really scared him because when he sees me coming, he looks very uncomfortable, turns around, and tries to avoid me.
>
> Therapist: So what made the difference was somehow you made up your mind not to tolerate his acting like nothing happened, and then you had the courage to do what you needed to do?
>
> Indira: Yes.
>
> Therapist: That is really remarkable.
>
> Indira: That's what she [gesturing toward the social worker] keeps telling me. She says I was really brave and really strong.
>
> Therapist: I think so, too.
>
> Indira: I know that's probably true, but I don't feel very brave or strong right now. I feel hopeless.
>
> Therapist: What do you think would need to happen in order for you to make a decision in this situation, and then to make your mind up to do whatever you needed to do?
>
> Indira: I don't know. I'm so scared. I don't feel very sure

of myself. I would need to be sure of myself and I'm not right now.

Therapist: On a scale of 0 to 10, with 0 meaning you have no confidence and 10 meaning you are completely sure of yourself, how sure of yourself do you imagine you would need to be in order to make a decision to do whatever you need to do?

Indira: Oh, at least an 8. A 9 would be great, but at least an 8.

Therapist: Where would you put yourself now on that scale?

Indira: Well maybe a half point because at least I'm here talking about it. But I'm not even at a 1.

Therapist: What would raise it even a little bit?

Indira: (Beginning to cry) I can't think of anything. I know you mean well, but this isn't working. Nothing is working. I need to be more sure of myself, but I haven't felt sure of myself even a little bit for a really long time. I always feel that someone other than me is in control. The only time I feel any control over my own life is at school and when I am alone cutting on myself. I'm not proud of it, but I cut on myself just before I came here. It was the only way I could think to comfort myself. I feel so ashamed. If I do marry, what will my husband think when he sees my bloody arms?

Therapist: It seems very understandable to me that you would want to comfort yourself at a time like this when you are facing such an important decision—to comfort yourself however you could. I am wondering what you did to comfort yourself when you were younger, before you were doing the cutting.

Indira: Well, I can't think of anything specific. Mostly I was a pretty happy kid. That was before the molestation started. I would go up to my room with a book, I guess. Get under the covers and it felt so safe and cozy. Sometimes I would take a nap in the afternoon with my mother in her bed. We each used to read until we fell asleep. I felt safe there. But it wasn't that unusual to feel that way, because I felt pretty comfortable all the time back then. I was a lot more sure of myself when I was little.

Therapist: *If you were to pick a time back then, perhaps even the one you were just talking about when you used to curl up on your bed with a book, and you were to put a number on that based on our scale, what would it be?*

Indira: *Oh, I was probably at an 8 at least, maybe even a 9 or a 10. Yes, some days back then I was definitely a 10. It probably sounds funny, but I hadn't learned yet what it means to be a girl. I thought I could do everything just like my brothers. It wasn't until I was eight or nine that I realized that all the rules were different for girls. After that everything seemed to change. I was still more or less happy, but I didn't feel I could do whatever I wanted to do. Before then, I really thought I could do anything. Not very realistic maybe, but I really believed in myself. I really had a sense of myself. (She smiled wistfully.)*

Therapist: *So let's suppose that somehow a miracle happened tonight while you were sleeping and when you awakened you believed in yourself and you thought you could do anything you needed to do. How would that affect your ability to make this decision? What would be the first thing that you would notice is different?*

Indira: *Well, I don't know which way I would decide, but I know I would feel secure when I woke up and I'd feel some confidence that when I did decide it would be in a way that was true to myself.*

Therapist: *How could you remind yourself of that 8 or 9 feeling like you had when you were a young girl? What would remind you or evoke that feeling for you, something you could carry with you while you are deciding?*

Indira: *I don't know why this comes to mind, but I have a little bracelet my parents gave me for my birthday right around the age I was talking about, before I knew that things were so different if you were a girl, when I still thought I could do anything. I haven't worn it for a long time.*

Therapist: *What would be the most useful, best message that the bracelet could stand for? Something that really would remind you of the 9 or 10 way of thinking?*

Indira: *Well, the bracelet would mean something like "I've got me, Indira. No matter what, I've got me." In fact, it has my initial attached to it. That would be the best message.*

Therapist: *So how confident are you that you can carry that bracelet and really do this, whatever you need to do to be true to yourself?*

Indira: *Oh, I can do it. I mean I can do it because I have to do it. I have no choice.*

The session ended with Indira smiling confidently. I confess I was somewhat shaken by her situation. It seemed like a very hard, complex set of decisions for such a young girl to have to navigate.

Indira returned for a follow-up consultation 10 days later. She looked serene and was smiling. When she returned home after our previous session, Indira had quietly telephoned several of her cousins and friends from her family's former village to find out what they knew about the prospective bridegroom. From all accounts he "sounded like a pretty good guy," very liberal in his thinking about women and careers, educated in the West, kind to his sisters and mother, with a good sense of humor, and quite good looking. She took this into consideration before talking to her mother.

She smiled as she began to tell the following story:

"I was so worried I didn't sleep much that night. I thought about cutting myself again, but I was so upset I couldn't even do that. The next morning, I waited until my father had gone to work and then went to my mother's room to talk with her. I was wearing the bracelet and holding the little initial with my other hand, holding onto it for dear life. I was so scared, I was shaking because I didn't know what my mother would say.

"I sat down across from her on the bed and I told her that I was willing to go back to [the native village] with her, and I would meet [the prospective bridegroom and his parents]. If he and I liked

*each other, I would agree to the marriage. But I also told her—
and this was very hard for me to say—if I didn't like him, I would
have to refuse. Also, I would only marry him under the following
conditions: I must be allowed to finish my education and to work
in my profession afterwards. I would be willing to live in a major
city in the U.S. or Europe as long as it has a good university. Certain cities would not be acceptable—Cleveland or Dallas, for example. And he and his parents must be told that if he ever beats
me or abuses me, I would leave and divorce him. He needs to understand that from the beginning."*

Indira said that her mother became very upset, and the talk had
ended with both of them in tears. However, later in the day she
went to Indira's room to speak with her. She told Indira that she
had thought it over and that she would talk to Indira's father about
what she had said. That night her mother talked with her father.
He was very angry, but Indira's mother prevailed and the prospective bridegroom's family was told of Indira's "conditions" before
Indira and her mother agreed to travel to the village.

Both families agreed on the conditions and Indira and her mother
were invited to travel to the bridegroom's home, where she would
meet him for the first time. If the couple liked each other, arrange-
ments would be made for the marriage to take place in the next year.

Indira looked at me with steady eyes. Her voice was calm, "I
know this must sound bizarre to you, but this is how things have
been done in my country for centuries. It is how my mother and
father met, my brothers and their wives, and my grandparents and
all of my cousins. I want it, too, but it has to be in a way that is
true to myself. I never want to lose the feeling of "I've got me,
Indira," again. I'm going to wear the bracelet when I meet him.
And if I like him and I decide to marry him, I'm going to pin it
inside my wedding dress."

She turned to her social worker, who had accompanied her to
this second consultation: "I cut myself just before I came today. But
before that I didn't cut myself for almost a week. I think I'm ready
to work on that now. It will be hard, but I know I'm going to have
to give it up. I don't want to have scarred arms. I want to wear
short-sleeved dresses. I want to work on this in our next session."

When Indira and I said goodbye, she was smiling broadly. I told
her, "You are a strong young woman." She replied, "I know. I have

to be. Look," she said, raising her arm so that her sweater fell back from her wrist. She was wearing the gold bracelet with the letter I on it.

SFBT can evoke resources within the client that can extend far beyond the imagination of the therapist. I would have never guessed how Indira could find a way to be true to herself despite these very complex cultural traditions. The assumption that Indira is competent enough to make the right decisions for herself permeates throughout the interview. For instance, it would have been very easy to try to talk Indira out of cutting herself, as the social worker had probably done (from a problem-solving stance). Instead, I communicated my admiration of her ability to deal with such a difficult dilemma through the questions I asked.

If clients identify an exception from long ago like Indira did, it is nice to invite them to create a concrete way of connecting the memory of the exception to future situations where they might need it. I like to rehearse this with clients by asking, "What do you think would be the best way to help yourself reconnect to that feeling (of confidence, security, etc.) when you most need it?" Usually the client will have a very unique way of doing this. Sometimes they decide to write it down, other times they choose to use something rich with symbolism, like Indira's bracelet.

All it took for Indira to discover her own resources was to remember her days of feeling competent, content, and happy with her life. Fortunately, Indira had experienced blissful periods in her young life, but even with clients whose lives seem to contain no successes or relief from suffering, it is still a good idea to ask about exceptions.

Indira's story is a very good example of how a therapist can take advantage of an unexpected event in a client's life and use it to transform her perspective of herself. Instead of looking at the marriage proposal as furthering and intensifying Indira's dilemma, as she herself saw it, Dolan helped Indira see this difficult situation as a way to transform and exert her sense of control over her future. The undiminished sense of respect for Indira's competence and her ability to shape her own future comes through in this interview. It is inspiring to witness such spinning of gold out of straw.

Chapter 4

MAPPING THE TERRITORY: STORIES ABOUT SCALING

Numbers are flexible and expandable. You can move up and down a numerical scale or multiply, divide, increase, or shrink a number. Words are not as flexible—in most languages a word stands for only one or two concepts. Thus, we find the scaling question the most versatile and useful tool; it is applicable in a variety of situations, with clients of different age, ethnicity, and presenting problems. When a client indicates a number, say 5, on the scale, we assume that he or she means somewhere in the middle, but we really don't know what the number means to this particular person. Only the client knows what the meaning of 5 holds for him or her. The beauty of the scaling question lies in the individual differences that we always strive to accommodate, respect, and capitalize on.

Most of all, we like scaling questions because numbers tend to be more neutral than words. For example, everybody can describe how certain events or meanings are connected to certain words, such as "your mother!"—which seem to have many layers of meaning. Of course, spouses and partners, parents and children know how to inflame or diffuse emotional intensity through the use of words. But people rarely fight about numbers. The use of numbers seems to trigger some cognitive ability to calmly observe or assess one's own situation and without responding emotionally to events, concepts, or emotions. Of course, there are limitless ways to adapt and use scaling questions. We find them particularly helpful in gauging:

- a client's progress in treatment
- a client's level of hopefulness
- how much energy a client has to invest in making life better
- how much trust, willingness, confidence, and motivation a client has

Here are some examples of using scaling questions with various problems:

- On a scale of 1 to 10, where 1 stands for how terribly confused you were when you first decided to call me and 10 stands for knowing what would make most sense to do about this situation, where would you say you are right now?
- At what number would you begin to feel like your fog is beginning to lift? What is the difference between 1 and 2? How can you tell that you have moved up from a 1 to a 2?
- What needs to happen so that you would feel like a 5?
- What would your daughter say if she were to explain how you have moved up from a 3 to a 5?
- Suppose 10 stands for how much you trusted your own judgment when you were confident about yourself. What tells you that you are at a 6 on this scale?
- Where do you need to be in order for you to feel able to get up in the morning?

In SFBT, scaling utilizes and incorporates the client's perceptions of what makes the problem better (as well as worse) into the process of therapeutic change. The various case stories in this chapter show how the scaling question can help clients to measure their own sense of their progress and to identify the next step they need to take in order to approach their goal.

Scaling questions are ideal for therapy with more than one person. Asking each person a scaling question regarding the therapy goal is a very effective way of respectfully including everyone in the session while maintaining a solid solution-oriented focus. The next case story illustrates how this can be done throughout the course of treatment.

Working Full-time with Pleasure
Contributed by Alasdair Macdonald, Carlisle, England

A home-care provider in her thirties, Verlene was urgently referred to our mental health service by her family doctor. Her husband, Joe, a policeman, attended the appointment with her. Their household also included their teenage son and a younger teenage daughter.

Verlene reported that she had taken a leave from work and had consulted her doctor because for six months she had been acutely afraid that she had AIDS and that others knew it. She had also developed fears that her husband wished her dead and was planning to poison her. Her sleep and concentration were poor. She believed that these fears were connected to a brief affair with a relative of her husband. The man in question had later killed himself following the break-up of another relationship. Her husband was aware of the affair, and Verlene and Joe had moved to another house to help end it.

Verlene explained that medication had improved her moods for up to half a day at a time. Joe's reassurance that he loved and needed her could relieve Verlene's distress for up to an hour. She described short-lived episodes of similar fear in the past, which had disappeared quickly after she discussed them with her husband.

On a scale of 1 to 10, with 10 signifying her feeling at her best, she rated herself at a 2. Her miracle would be to return to full-time work (a respiratory disease recently had required her to drop to part-time), to lose her distressing fears, do more things with her husband, and to be able to be supportive of her children. At the end of the session, I complimented Verlene and Joe on the effort they had both put into overcoming the difficulties in their immediate family and the strains on their relationship. I remarked that both of their jobs entailed working hard to support other people. I suggested that recent events had caused them more fatigue than *they had recognized and that it would be wise to think about changes, but not to make any yet.* [*]

A month later Verlene and Joe attended another session. She had achieved her goal of going out once with Joe and had extended this to include going out once a day with the dog or with a friend. I asked both Verlene and Joe to rate Verlene on the scale. By inviting Joe to participate in the scaling, I hoped to provide Verlene with additional real-life opportunities for validation and encouragement. She felt she was at a 3 on the scale and he thought she might be at a 4, indicating that Joe saw more hopeful signs about Verlene than she did herself. The next steps that she identified were to start fitness training again or to go swimming. Joe was going away for a week and she was worried about coping with her daughter during that time.

Five weeks later the couple returned. Verlene had coped successfully with the children and the household during her husband's absence. She had not yet been to fitness classes. Both Verlene and Joe felt that she was at a 5 on the scale. The next step she identified was to visit friends instead of having them come to her home. She asked Joe to start working out with her and planned to later continue working out on her own. They also planned to resume going out together socially.

Six months later Verlene felt that she had slipped backwards, that everything seemed to be going wrong, and she began to recount her failures. She had attempted to keep fit and go swimming but had sprained her ankle, which had prevented further activity. She had not been able to visit her friend because she thought she detected reluctance in her friend's voice on the phone. One night

---

[*] A rather curious but common occurrence is the gradual disappearance of the client's initial presenting complaint, such as Verlene's fears of AIDS or being poisoned by her loved ones, when we do not pay undue attention to it. If one were to work from the "problem-solving" mind-set, it would seem logical to keep track of these rather serious presenting problems; however, in SFBT, as client and therapist focus on the more successful side of the client's life, these complaints seem to disappear. While we have no logical, convincing explanation for this phenomenon, my (IKB) clinical hunch is that the more clients talk about their successes, the more these successes seem to preoccupy their mind and energy. It has occurred to many SFBT advocates, such as Gale Miller and Steve de Shazer (2000), that language plays a key role in creating a different reality.

after they had had too much to drink, Verlene and Joe quarreled. Verlene felt that Joe had been taking less interest in her, and Joe felt that she had been less interested in him. The recent death of their daughter's previous boyfriend had also caused stress in the family. Both Verlene and Joe agreed she was at a 5 on the scale. She identified the next step as resuming her fitness program once her ankle healed.

At the end of the session, I highlighted the progress that Verlene and Joe had made and the fact that they maintained a 5 in spite of disagreements and their daughter's bereavement. I complimented them on their ability to act together in relation to the children and to share appropriate plans for the future. I advised them again not to make changes at this point in view of the current external stresses in their life.

A month later, Verlene had coped successfully while Joe was away on a trip. They had been swimming together, had gone on a 14-mile walk, and agreed to jointly work on losing weight. In addition, they had also come to an agreement with the children to reduce arguments at home. Verlene rated herself at a 6 on the scale and thought that her next step would be to take more interest in Joe's work and activities. I complimented them again on their ability to work together. I said that their ability to cooperate regarding their children was evidence of good parenting skills. I confirmed that they would know when the time for the next steps had come.

Two months later, Verlene and Joe had been on holiday successfully. Their daughter's behavior during the holiday had been excellent. Verlene was at a 6.5 on the progress scale. She believed that the next step would be to keep fit and to consider returning to work. I congratulated them on the improvement in their daughter's behavior. I agreed that it was a good idea for them to follow their plan of examining whether a partial return to work would affect their financial situation.

Another two months later, Verlene had resumed work on a part-time basis. She was sleeping well and felt that she was back to her old self. She had been driving and taking part in her usual activities. Both Verlene and Joe placed her at a 7 on the scale. I complimented them on their good progress and the possibility of terminating therapy was discussed. They felt that one more appointment would be appropriate.

Unfortunately, when I saw Verlene three months later, she had developed health symptoms that indicated she might have a tumor. She had continued to work in spite of her symptoms but was undergoing extensive medical and neurological tests. There had also been disagreements between the couple and Joe's relatives. Verlene felt that she was now at a 6 on the scale, although Joe felt that she was closer to a 7. She thought that she could not move forward until the results of the medical tests were available, which would be in a month. I agreed that they were coping well and maintaining progress in the face of very difficult circumstances. I suggested that it was wise not to plan anything new until Verlene's physical health had been appropriately assessed.

Three months later, no life-threatening cause had been found for Verlene's symptoms, though some medical tests still needed to be done. There had been no further family disagreements. Verlene was taking a small dose of antidepressants and was happily working six days a week, but the couple still had not begun fitness training. They both agreed that Verlene was at a 7 on the scale. They felt that a sign of progress would be the continued absence of family disagreements. They also believed that if disagreements should occur, they would be able to resolve them successfully. I complimented them on their good progress in the face of these difficulties. They felt that one more appointment was necessary.

Three months later, Verlene and Joe reported that Verlene was working full-time and that they had had another successful family holiday. They had reached a mutual decision to eventually move to another part of the country, as promotion for Joe was more likely if he was prepared to move. Verlene's physical health had improved and she was able to work six days a week without difficulty. Both agreed that she was at an 8 on the scale and that this had been sustained for some time. They felt that further appointments were unnecessary.

In the final session, I highlighted the many difficulties they had overcome, as well as the initial presenting symptoms. I congratulated them on their close marriage, their shared activities, and their parenting skills.

A Little Piece of Paper
Contributed by Britta Severin, Malmo, Sweden

It's difficult for many to imagine working with someone who is aggressive, has a history of being violent toward his partner, and is determined to revenge what he views as the wrongs done to him. Britta Severin has successfully worked with such a person. In contrast to her client's reputation and demeanor, Britta is soft-spoken and low-keyed. These two contrasting characters manage to work together in the following story, using only one tool: the scaling question.

I work as a probation officer, and one of my clients, Johann, was in prison when I first met him. He had been sentenced for assault, unlawful threat, and interference in a judicial matter, and he was soon to be released on condition that he be supervised for two years. He had a long list of convictions for assault and unlawful threat prior to his current prison sentence.

A judge had ordered that Johann be given a thorough psychiatric evaluation, and he had been characterized as paranoid, explosive, and antisocial, with an extremely low tolerance for frustration. The evaluation revealed that Johann had been given strong psychopharmaceutical medications as a child, and that as an adult he had become aggressive and threatening. Johann previously had been seen by many different psychiatrists and psychologists, and under coercion he had been treated in psychiatric hospitals for his progressive behavioral problems.

When the prison officer went to get Johann for our first meeting, Johann sent the officer back with the message that he did not want to see me. So I decided to go to see Johann at the prison workshop. When someone from outside the prison system visits a prison workshop, it causes a stir. Everyone looks up at the visitor and calls out loud, mostly unflattering, comments. When I approached Johann in the prison workshop, he told me that he had nothing to talk about. I responded, "That's possible, but I have a couple things that I need to talk to you about, as you are to be on parole and I am your parole officer for the next two years." This is how our relationship began.

Johann and his ex-wife, Anne, had a little son, Eric, who was living with his mother. But because of Johann's behavior (he had been sentenced for threatening and beating Anne), a restraining order had been placed against him. This was very painful for Johann, who was deeply wounded at the thought of not being able to see his young son. While he was still in prison, Johann went to the appellate court to see if the restraining order could be lifted so that he could see his son. The appellate court denied his petition. Later, Johann confided to me that he had gone to court tranquilized. Because he knew Anne would be there and didn't want to risk not being able to control himself, he thought the tranquilizer was a good idea. He was pleasantly surprised when I complimented him on this decision to show his effort to control his behavior, he said I was the first person he had met who thought it wise to take tranquilizers. But it was clear that he was pleased with my recognition of his effort.

For the first few sessions (beginning in prison and then shortly after his release), Johann talked primarily about how he wanted to take revenge on Anne and torment her. He said he wanted to spare me the details of his plan, but he was preoccupied by these thoughts. He told me that he thought about it from the time he woke up in the morning until he fell asleep at night. When I asked him to scale his life, with 10 standing for how he wanted his to be, he scaled himself at 0.

After meeting with Johann for several times, I commented that although he was preoccupied with thoughts of revenge he did not carry them out, and that there was a difference between doing and thinking. It was a catch-22 for him, he said, because although he wanted revenge, he also was tormented by the constant presence of his revenge fantasies.

A few sessions later, I discovered an exception that I could focus on in our visits. Johann was complaining about a pain in his shoulder. When I asked about the pain, he explained that he had been having a beer in a pub when a man approached him, took his drink, and pushed him so hard that he fell off the stool. I was concerned and asked, "What did you do?" Johann replied, "Nothing. I was sober."

I was struck by this. Having been repeatedly charged with assault, Johann had previously described himself as someone who

*was aggressive and could not control himself. And yet he had done
"nothing" this time when he was provoked! I was very curious
about how Johann had accomplished this and was intrigued by the
fact that being sober had helped. I also was interested in what else
had helped Johann to accomplish this.*

*Johann suggested that he was in a more balanced psychological
state than he had been in the past. I wondered aloud about what
he had done to achieve this balance and he told me that he had already done quite a lot. He had fixed up his apartment, had contacted an employment agency about a course or a job, and was
taking steps to pay off his debts. He also had been seeing his two
teenage children from his first marriage. Furthermore, he had
started jogging!*

*When asked to scale himself again, 0 to 10, where 10 stood for
how he wanted his life to be, he answered as 7. I agreed with
Johann that he had indeed come a long way from when he left the
prison, and told him so. Even though Johann is not an openly ex-
pressive person, it was easy to see that he was very pleased with
compliments and was more accepting of them because they were
based on his achievements and accomplishments.*

*Subsequently, Johann got a job. He saw his teenage children of-
ten. When I asked how he reached this decision to make changes
and behave differently, Johann said it was for the sake of his children, that he wanted to stay in shape, not ruminate so much, and
be more available emotionally. Seeing his older children made him
realize that although he wanted to hurt his ex-wife, he didn't want
his children to have a murderer for a father.*

*Johann also began to have contact with Karen, the mother of
his teenage children. Johann and Karen had separated many years
before and maintained a cooperative relationship. The children
lived with Karen, and Johann was welcome in their home. As
Johann's life began to balance, Karen obviously trusted him and
allowed the children to spend weekends with him.*

*One day Johann came in to see me voluntarily and reported that
on the scale of 0 to 10, he was at a minus 273! I swallowed hard
and tried to stay calm. When I asked him what was wrong, he
reported feeling depressed because his coworkers had made deroga-
tory remarks about his having been a "jail bird" and tried to*

provoke him into a fight that he knew he must not get into. He thought that this experience of his surging anger and passing thoughts to harm these guys was a great setback in the hard work he had put into maintaining his balance since his release from prison. I was relieved that he did not get into an actual fight but was able to walk away from them. In order to help him gain some perspective on his year-long achievement, I asked him if he felt that anything was better in his life than it was a year ago.

Johann replied that yes, some things were better. He had managed to stay away from Anne, he had not committed any crimes, and he had found he could keep quiet. He had spent a lot of time with his teenage children and on one occasion he and Karen had consulted a counselor when one of the children had a problem. He realized that he was important as a father, and this had stopped him from committing suicide. He realized he didn't want to keep his hatred. He wanted to go on with his life—to continue doing things that were good for him with the hope of being able to see his son someday.

As time went on, Johann continued to see his teenage children and improve his life and behavior. Just after successfully completing his two-year court-ordered supervision period, Johann contacted me to schedule an appointment. Early in my relationship with Johann as his parole officer, he had given me a little piece of paper on which he had written Anne's address. Johann now asked me to write a letter confirming that, although Johann had known Anne's address since his release from prison two years ago (which the piece of paper proved), he had made no attempt to see her. Johann hoped this would help him appeal for permission to see his son.

This gesture perfectly illustrated the profound changes Johann had made. He had taken control of his life and gone from being aggressive and threatening to being a man who respected other people and received respect in return. He had become a caring father for his older children and observed the restraining order put against him. Now a calm and realistic person capable of making plans for his future, he was able to begin working toward a visitation arrangement that would be best for him and Eric.

Chapter 5

"WOW! HOW DID YOU DO THAT?": STORIES ABOUT COMPLIMENTS AS INTERVENTIONS

We think that all talking between the client and therapist is potentially interventive. Contrary to what most people believe—that interviewing means gathering information in order to formulate the problems and prescriptive interventions—we believe that questions not only influence what the client notices and pays attention to, but also shape the answers we get. Therefore, the subtle phrasing of questions determines the interaction between the therapist and clients.

As was noted in chapter 1, there is a great deal of difference between a question about "why" a client did something and a question about "how" the client did it. Not surprisingly, most clients are sensitive enough to notice the difference between "why" and "how," and respond accordingly. Described as "admiring commiseration" (Janet Beavin Bevales, personal communication, 1998), "How did you do it?" states that "you already have done it, I just want to know *how* you did it." Answers to this question elicit client competence and accomplishment and then focus on it. Of course, the more the doctor asks exploratory questions ("Tell me again about how you stopped smoking?" or "Wasn't it hard to do? Most of my patients find it very hard to stop smoking. What do you suppose you did that worked for you?"), the more the conversation becomes complimentary. "How did you know that changing the place where you drank your after-dinner coffee would make such a difference in your determination to stop smoking?"

Listen to the differences the following questions could generate:

- Have you ever had a job before?
- What kind of jobs have you had before?
- How many jobs have you had before?

These questions not only convey information about the practitioner's preformed impression of the client while obtaining information from the client, but also generate entirely different responses that the counselor can pursue. "Have you ever had a job before?" can be heard by the job seeker as rather demeaning. Furthermore, questions that ask for factual accounts or can be answered with a "yes" or "no" are limiting and close the conversation. On the other hand, "What kind of jobs have you had before?" invites clients to show off how many different skills they may have, how they went about getting different jobs, how long they stayed on one job compared to another, and so on. This type of conversation provides the counselor with a great deal of information about the client as well as giving information to the client about the counselor's interest in him or her.

Of all the compliments that come up in conversation, we believe the "self-compliment" has the most powerful impact in validating the client's own successes and competencies. After all, what *we* say stays with us longer than what we heard someone say *to* us. Therefore, we believe that the most useful "compliment" therapists can give is to ask questions that allow clients to formulate answers more complex than a simple "yes" or "no." In the process of answering, clients are literally spinning yarns of competence, goodwill, and good intentions. Things become clearer as they try to articulate something they have been only vaguely aware of. By putting into words something about which they just had a hunch, they are able to name it and look at it.

The client/therapist conversation is always an exchange of information that goes in both directions. Without realizing it, many therapists give clues about what they think of the client. The client responds, often without even being aware of it. It is crucial that our perception, attitude, and stance toward the client are very clear and positive, because they can easily slip out. Of course, raising an eyebrow, changing your tone of voice, opening your eyes wide, or leaning forward to get more information all convey to the client that you admire his or her courage, fortitude, and impressive accomplishments. Since this kind of exchange of information is inevitable, why not use it deliberately, more thoughtfully, and to the benefit of the client? That's how language—verbal and nonverbal—works, and language is the single most important tool we use in our daily work.

Isabel's Story:
Using SFBT to Treat Obsessive-Compulsive Disorder
Contributed by Luc Isebaert, M.D., Brugge, Belgium

Eliciting client competence means allowing clients to navigate their own ways of reaching their goals. This requires therapists to forsake the hierarchical relationship traditionally held between them and their clients. Leveling the playing field like this often produces astoundingly positive results, particularly with clients who are used to being told what is "best" for them rather than figuring it out on their own, like the woman in this story.

Isabel was a pleasant-looking 48-year-old woman who had raised two sons who were now away at college. Her husband of 23 years was very helpful and attentive to her demands.

At our first meeting, Isabel explained that her problem started when she was diagnosed with obsessive-compulsive disorder four years earlier. She had been taken to a hospital because of her acute symptoms, an obsession with cleanliness and fear of contamination. She was unable to take a bath alone because she feared the water and worried that her soap might transmit germs. She repeatedly checked everything in her household: the ashtrays she had just emptied, the coffee cups and wastebaskets, the dishes she had washed by hand because the dishwasher might not wash them properly, and so on.

Isabel had an endless list of germs and dirt, and everything in her environment was a possible source of danger. Life became very exhausting and Isabel couldn't get her work done. Furthermore, her fear of contamination made it impossible for her to leave the house. Her social life became increasingly restricted because she was unable to visit friends or to have them over to the house.

Isabel said that she had already tried desensitization and other behavioral programs but had relapsed quickly. She was not interested in trying the same thing again. She agreed to be hospitalized this time only on the condition that I would not force a behavioral program upon her. I consented. I told Isabel that while she was in the hospital, "you should do nothing you cannot do." I concentrated on asking her coping questions, and I complimented her on the things that she was able to do, such as taking a bath when a female nurse was sitting with her and eating a meal on her own. Eventually she was discharged from the hospital.

Following the discharge, Isabel saw me twice a week, and we gradually reduced the frequency to once a week. In our conversation during these sessions we never focused on what she should do, but rather tried to discover what she already was able to do on her own. I continued to compliment her on the things she was able to do, such as taking a bath with someone sitting next to her or going for a walk with her sister.

Three months after her discharge from the hospital, Isabel's husband left her for another woman, explaining that now that she was doing better, he could finally leave her. Somehow, her husband's leaving did not prompt Isabel to relapse. Perhaps she gained strength from the fact that she had a very supportive family and caring friends. Her brother telephoned every day to check on how she was doing. Her sister stopped by to visit every day. She usually brought biscuits, and she and Isabel would spend the afternoon drinking coffee and chatting about everyday things. During these visits with her sister, Isabel was able to take a bath. Isabel's neighbors helped with various household chores and took care of outdoor tasks. Her sons stayed busy with their lives and were not involved in her care, but she rarely complained about them.

A turning point came two years after Isabel's discharge from the hospital. Six weeks of hot summer weather had kept the temperature *unrelentingly high. Isabel's sister had been unable to visit as often because she was caring for their mother, whose heart condition caused her to suffer from the heat. After going three weeks without a bath because of her sister's absence, Isabel began to notice that she was becoming rather smelly. Finally, she could no longer stand herself. She described what she had done: "I closed my eyes, jumped into the tub, and took my bath all alone." Although I was very tempted to encourage Isabel to continue this new accomplishment of bathing by herself, I refrained and instead reminded her that she might still need her sister to come and sit with her.*

The finalization of her divorce was traumatic for Isabel. She still loved her husband very much. In addition, their house had to be sold, and she had to move to a smaller house because that was what she could afford. Isabel started doing household chores on her own. She joined a singles club and participated in various activities every week. Eventually we reduced the frequency of her sessions to once every six to eight weeks. She always began each session with,

Isabel: Doctor, I've done pretty well.

Doctor: Oh?

Isabel: Yes, I've decided to move back to the village where I was raised.

Doctor: That seems like a big decision.

Isabel: Yes, it is, but I decided that I really don't need a big house anymore because there is only myself. I want to go back to my roots, where I was raised. I can afford to have my own place in the village and my aunts and uncles are still living there. It will be good for my mother to visit me there, too.

Doctor: That was a big decision to make. How were you able to make such an important decision and still keep up your progress?

Isabel: I keep thinking I have to grow up someday and I need to become more independent—my mother and my sister will not live forever, you know.

Doctor: I have no doubt that is true. So, how are you able to keep making progress?

> Isabel: I talk to myself everyday, several times a day.
> Doctor: So, are you getting better at listening to yourself, too?
> Isabel: I guess I am better at listening to my own advice.

Isabel continued to improve even as she went through these changes. I continued to compliment her on the numerous accomplishments she reported in each session, including the steps she had to take to move back to the village—sorting and packing her belongings, and allowing the potential buyer to inspect her house. Even though she was quite stressed, with much support from her family and neighbors she was able to maintain her gains without a setback, which was remarkable for Isabel.

During the final session, I asked her to reflect on her progress and the course of treatment this time compared to her other hospitalization and therapy. She replied that her past treatment had pushed her too much and too quickly.

Clients with obsessive-compulsive disorder are often considered "resistant" and difficult to treat. Some therapists even say these patients are "too difficult" to work with. In working with this population over the years, I have found that people with a tendency toward obsessive-compulsive behavior cannot imagine the future; they can only see present and past successes. Therefore, negotiating future goals is meaningless to them. This is often perceived as "resistance."

It also seems important not to push, suggest, or encourage them to repeat successful behaviors or to take the next step. My thinking is that most people with this kind of dilemma prefer to not define or participate in a relationship that is essentially hierarchical. They tend to shy away from taking and following advice and accepting encouragement, because it entails maintaining a hierarchical relationship in which the psychotherapist is in a dominant position.

Isebaert's view that the therapist avoid a dominant hierarchical position is very wise. Of course, such a stance requires a good measure of psychological sophistication and maturity (in order to resist the temptation to offer encouragement or advice), as well as solid clinical expertise and relational ability. I (IKB) am often asked by students and new therapists about my patience and my ability to sit still in long silences during interviews when there seems to be no activity with clients. Many people seem to have the idea that brief therapy means "short" or cutting long-term therapy into short segments and calling them "brief." In fact, at times "going slow" seems to get you there faster. I believe that in order to work briefly, one needs to learn to slow down, to be patient, and as Isebaert has done with Isabel, take the time. But most of all, grow a big ear, listen carefully for the small kernels of success, and inject hope. Hope is the greatest gift we can offer our clients.

Fear of Swallowing: Using SFBT in an Inpatient Setting
Contributed by Anne Lutz, M.D., Boston, Massachusetts

Through direct and indirect compliments, as well as through non-verbal complimentary communication, the therapist establishes a rapport with the client that is delicately balanced and consistently sensitive to the client's needs and goals. The agenda of the SFBT therapist is the agenda the client sets for him- or herself. In an inpatient setting, however, this balance may be easily upset, as many professionals and caregivers with possibly different agendas interact with the patient.

Working in an inpatient setting seems to require a whole different set of skills. Although doctors must carry considerable responsibility for management of cases, their approach can still be very solution-focused, as this story demonstrates. "I try to acknowledge the nurses on my team and include them," Lutz says. "I ask them their ideas as well as offering them my ideas. If some staff disagrees with my ideas, I never 'confront' them but instead acknowledge their ideas and efforts, then find a small piece that we agree on and basically still carry out the main piece of work I wanted to do anyway. I never disagree with supervisors but try to find small ways to compliment the team of doctors. They then seem more able to listen to my thoughts. So, I try to say less instead of trying to explain more about the details of what I do and think." In this case, Lutz cooperated with the entire staff in order to help Claire and her parents.

Claire was an 11-year-old girl who was admitted to the inpatient psychiatric unit after being transferred from the medical unit. She had been treated on the medical ward to stabilize the dehydration that developed as a result of her refusal to eat, drink, or swallow her saliva for the preceding three months. Her parents, Beth and Michael, described her as a top student and a model child, involved in many activities including violin, basketball, softball, and ballet. She and her twin brother were to begin middle school in the fall. This was her first hospitalization, and her past medical history was noncontributory except for a tonsillectomy. There was no history of trauma.

Claire had lost a total of about 20 pounds, a great deal of weight for a child her age. Her parents explained that her difficulties had started after she had contracted a stomach virus. They had taken her to a pediatrician, who referred her for a battery of tests, including an upper gastrointestinal (GI) series, an electrogastrogram, an upper GI endoscopy with biopsies, a head MRI, bloodwork studies, and trials of several stomach medications. All the tests indicated that she was normal.

Beth and Michael reported that after the stomach virus, Claire began to slowly restrict her eating, complained of energy loss, became increasingly anxious, and developed fears about germs and needles. Two weeks before the hospital admission, she began refusing to swallow her own saliva. Her parents started spoon-feeding her. Claire said she didn't vomit, use laxatives, or fear gaining weight. She did not view herself as fat. Her family background included a paternal history of panic attacks and ADHD, a paternal aunt with a history of depression, and a maternal history of obsessive-compulsive disorder.

I first saw Claire on the medical unit, following the medical team's request for a consultation, because they were concerned about a "behavioral component" in her difficulties. During the first meeting, Claire sat in a hospital bed and was fed through a nasogastric tube. She initially refused to talk. Her mother stayed at her bedside, repeatedly stroking her daughter's forehead and arms.

Beth was obviously very worried about Claire. She wanted to understand what was troubling her daughter and discover what she was "repressing." She wanted Claire to be medically safe and get back to a "normal life of eating and socializing."

She had tried numerous ways of helping her daughter, none of which had proved useful. They included "encouraging her to talk about her feelings," taking her to a therapist (with whom Claire refused to talk), and, most recently, resorting to spoon-feeding her.

When Claire stabilized medically, she was transferred to the in-patient psychiatric unit where I worked. A thin child in a wheelchair with a nasogastric tube in place, she held a plastic cup into which she would intermittently spit her saliva. She had poor eye contact and refused to talk with the staff, only whispering softly to her mother. Occasionally, Claire would write her answers to questions on paper. She appeared tearful and anxious around her parents, which was most of the day. There was no evidence of suicidal, psychotic, or homicidal ideation.

A marked change in Claire's behavior occurred after her parents left the unit. Claire talked normally to her peers, did not carry a cup to spit into, and even smiled. When we asked the miracle question she responded by saying she would like to feel hungry, eat more, see her parents happy, and be able to feed herself. On a scale of 1 to 10, with 10 representing her desired state, Claire rated herself at a 3. She explained that she was not a 1 because she was "trying to eat." She was able to identify how her life was different and better before her eating and swallowing problems started. She talked about school, feeling good, feeling hungry, and doing "fun things" like sports and music.

Based on our observation of Claire's sudden behavioral changes when her parents left the unit, the staff agreed that Claire's case needed to move toward separation between the mother and the child. My conversation with the staff was on how to help the parents realize that their absence was helping Claire but do it without blaming them. This was difficult to do because the parents became anxious when they were separated from Claire and because Beth was a very sensitive person. We decided to create a structured visiting plan. While implementing this, we offered Beth and Michael many compliments on their strength in being able to leave their daughter in the hospital and tolerate their own anxiety. We reassured them by telling them how obvious it was that they loved their daughter very much. We encouraged them to notice what they were doing differently that could account for the improvements Claire was making and to imagine what things would be like as she became an adolescent. For example, how would they know when she was ready for dating? What about driving a car? They were also complimented on their ability to care for twins—not an easy task. They acknowledged that they had felt guilty about not having enough time for each infant.

We also complimented Beth and Michael on their ability to have such close supportive relationships with their children. We asked how they were able to do this, and how they knew when their children were ready to move to the next developmental stage.

The staff complimented Beth on her ability to let Claire bathe and wash her hair alone. This was something she previously had been doing for Claire. We noted the obvious commitment and love the parents had for their children, as well as their ability to work together to solve this problem. The staff made a point of observing the times when Beth and Michael were interacting with Claire in an age-appropriate manner. This gave us more opportunities to compliment the whole family on their maturity at being able to plan and carry out activities everyone could enjoy.

Individual sessions with Claire centered around complimenting her and noticing ways in which she was doing things differently. Claire was complimented on her choice to drink Ensure rather than receiving food through the tube. The staff attempted to facilitate her independence and support her having the strength to eat by making comments like "Wow, how were you able to drink that sip of Ensure?" and "You have so much determination and strength to be able to do this." They also complimented her on walking rather than using the wheelchair, talking in audible tones rather than whispering, washing her own hair, and participating in group activities.

During a family meeting, Claire voiced a desire to start playing hockey with her father and brother, something she had always wanted to do but never had done. Beth and Michael were able to allow this even though they had always believed that Claire would rather take ballet and ice skating. We complimented Claire on her *increasing independence and her strength in asserting herself. I continued to use scaling questions in both individual and family sessions to assess her sense of independence. As time progressed, the number gradually went up from a 1 (on the day I met her) to a 10 (on the day of her discharge).*

After her discharge from the hospital, Claire and her family were followed on an outpatient basis. She continued to improve and Beth became very good at noticing developmentally appropriate progress. Beth began to compliment Claire on her ability to go to school, have her own locker, say goodbye to grade school, and other behaviors normal for an 11-year-old. I complimented Beth on her increasing ability to give credit to her daughter, a sign that she was indeed becoming very skilled at being the parent of a preadolescent.

At our final session, Beth expressed how she and Michael were worried about possible refusal to go to school based on Claire's past problems with separation anxiety, but they made it known in no uncertain terms that at any such indication from Claire they were prepared to send her away to a boarding school because the law required her to be in school. They also told Claire that if she chose not to eat, they would not hesitate to bring her back to the hospital, because they would not allow her to risk her own health and safety again.

Complimenting only the successful steps a client is taking seems simple—too simple in fact. Couldn't anybody, with or without clinical training, do it? And how can it work with such a complicated case as Claire's? Giving compliments actually requires good clinical judgment and timing. Compliments must point toward what to do more, not what to eliminate or stop doing. Many people know what is wrong or when the problem is bothering them but have run out of ideas about what to do instead of repeating the same ineffective solutions. Even the most supportive parents, who wish nothing but the best for their children, such as Beth and Michael, are often at a loss when it comes to knowing what will work. Both direct and indirect compliments spotlight nascent successful strategies and keep clients focused on those that work.

A Tired Mother and a Deep Breath:
Exceptions and Compliments
Contributed by Aviva Holmqvist, Malmo, Sweden

Helping clients find exceptions to their problems is in itself a subtle way of complimenting them. By assuming that an exception exists, you send the message that the client can—in fact, has already begun to—solve the problem. The story of Marit and Lisa illustrates this.

A social worker in the process of investigating a foster care placement referred 12-year-old Lisa and her mother Marit to our agency. She wanted help in finding a way for them to continue living together. Marit felt she couldn't cope with Lisa anymore. Marit's ex-husband was a drug addict, so she bore the responsibility of raising Lisa and her other daughter Sheila (5 years old) on her own.

Marit and Lisa each had regularly been seeing individual therapists at a children's psychiatric unit for at least a year. Marit herself had been a "social services kid." She had been placed in a series of foster homes as a child and had been treated at the same children's psychiatric unit where her daughter was now being seen. The family was "well known in the social services" because of their long-term involvement with various services. Lisa had already been assigned a "support family" and spent every weekend and almost every night there instead of at home with her mother. She had developed nervous ticks and an assortment of phobias and had a history of cutting her wrists and choking herself. She screamed that she wanted to die during her frequent fights with Marit, and she repeatedly telephoned the social services agency in the evenings threatening to kill herself.

At her wit's end, Marit had recently asked to place Lisa in a foster home. Marit had informed Lisa on the way to our first session that the social worker intended to place her in foster care as soon as possible, even before Christmas, which was only three weeks away. In the session, Lisa started crying and shouting at her mother, who reacted by appearing increasingly tired and withdrawn. In response to Lisa's accusations, Marit repeated that it wasn't up to her, that she would like to help Lisa but she was too tired and that maybe there was something wrong with Lisa's hormones. As this continued, Lisa became angrier and angrier and finally screamed at Marit, "You are the worst mother there is, you can't do anything! I hate you, I hate you! I wish you were dead."

I (along with an SFBT team) was supervising the therapy from behind a mirror. Realizing that the therapist was having serious difficulties, I interrupted the session by walking into the room and introducing myself as a team member, though this is not my usual way of supervising.

I told Marit and Lisa that it was obvious to the team behind the mirror how much they loved each other and really wanted things to work out. I added that the team could also see how hurt and disappointed both of them were, how tired Marit was, and how desperate Lisa felt. I added that in my experience people who love each other and are feeling hurt say a lot of horrible things they don't mean, just as Marit and Lisa were doing, and that the team would really like to try to help them "work things out" (Marit and Lisa's general description of their goal).

I asked if during the previous two weeks (since they had last seen a therapist) there had been any moments when they had done something together other than fight. Lo and behold, a miracle happened! Lisa and Marit said that 4 of the past 14 days had been good. Not only had they abstained from fighting, but there also had been moments when Lisa was tempted to shout at her mother but listened when her mother said, "Let's not do this, Lisa." Following this exchange, Lisa had gone to her room and withdrawn for a while. On one occasion after Lisa had been in her room for a while Marit had joined her and they spent a pleasant moment together. Marit also remembered that Lisa had listened to her and had avoided fighting with Sheila.

Encouraged by the new direction of the session, Lisa and Marit went on to describe the positive effect these behaviors had on each other. Lisa noticed that Marit had more patience and more energy, and Marit noticed that Lisa appeared happier and more obliging. Lisa had, in fact, offered to help Marit clean up and had offered to sleep at her aunt's one evening when she saw how tired her mother was. This was the first time Marit was aware that Lisa noticed her fatigue and tried to be considerate.

I then focused on helping Marit think of other exceptions to the problem. She mentioned times like decorating for Christmas together and going to town to see the holiday window decorations. We discussed how Lisa had managed to keep the temptation to fight at bay, and how Marit had managed to notice Lisa's attempts to do this, despite her fatigue and hopelessness.

A very articulate and observant child, Lisa confided that when she felt the itch to fight she tried to get out of the way until she calmed down. Marit tried to help by commenting that she thought a fight was about to start and by letting Lisa go to her room and calm down before going in to see her.

At this point in the session, Lisa seemed to have more available energy than her mother to take another little step in the right direction. Marit said that she was beginning "to see the light at the end of the tunnel," but at this point she couldn't think of anything else that she had the strength to do. She said she needed to take each day as it came. She did, however, feel that she would get more strength once she saw Lisa taking another step forward.

Our team took a consultation break and then talked with Marit and Lisa. We mentioned again that we could see that Marit and Lisa were obviously very important to each other, and we sensed how painful it was for the two of them to be unable to reach each other. We said that we were impressed by their four successful days and were curious about how they had succeeded in creating these "oases."

We acknowledged to Lisa that it was difficult for a 12-year-old to take the responsibility for the next step, but emphasized that, as we saw it, Marit currently did not have the strength. Therefore, we asked Lisa to carefully observe the times she managed to avoid letting the fights take over and to notice what she did instead.

We had two more sessions with Lisa and Marit after this. By the second session, Marit and Lisa's fighting problem was solved. Lisa had managed to avoid most of the fights, and Marit expressed joy that her daughter was being so considerate. Marit also apologized to Lisa for putting the responsibility on her.

In the final session, we asked Lisa and Marit to discuss what advice we should give other families in their situation. Both agreed that it was important to walk away instead of fighting and to do pleasant things together. At this point, Marit and Lisa and our team mutually agreed to terminate therapy. The referring social worker was satisfied, too. Contact between Marit and Lisa and the social services was terminated two months after therapy ended. This was the first time in years that the family was not involved with social services.

Unbelievable? I followed up with Marit and Lisa during the subsequent five years. Today Lisa is a lovely, mature 17-year-old. She has done well at school and is studying design and media. Marit has completed her grade school equivalency and was on her way to graduating from high school when the Swedish economy collapsed. The state ordered students to begin paying back government-issued loans immediately, and she was forced to interrupt her education.

In a recent interview, Marit and Lisa said that they have had their arguments but they always remember that they basically love each other no matter what. Lisa has been living with her aunt and uncle for the past two months. This decision was made jointly by Lisa and Marit. They see each other every day and Lisa stays at her mother's house whenever she feels like it. This is working very well for both of them.

When I asked about their experience in therapy with the SFBT team, Lisa and Marit had different views. Lisa said she didn't remember coming to the team and that "maybe I've denied it and should think about it." To this, I responded that not remembering therapy is a very good sign; therapy should only be a parentheses in one's life. Marit said that the first session was what made the difference: "When parents give up they don't have anyone who comes in and says there is something. . . . You said we loved each other so much that we hated each other. You were so positive all the time, so I started thinking this is something to hold onto. . . . I've done some good things for my children. What can I do to go on? And I started to think about the positive instead of the negative. For the first time I could take a deep breath. This *helped us in other difficult periods, knowing we were doing well together."*

At this point, Marit observed, *"Why dig up the past? It's over . . . each person must find their own solutions."* She concluded, *"You saw the present and encouraged us."*

The team in this case was very skilled both at identifying Marit and Lisa's strengths in a reassuring manner and especially at identifying and utilizing the exceptions to the problem. This must have been especially challenging during the first session, when Marit and Lisa were in a state of crisis. By complimenting them both on their love for each other and their desire to "work things out," the team successfully intervened in what was becoming an increasingly damaging exchange. By refocusing the session, they also encouraged Marit and Lisa to value each other, which ultimately provided them with an alternative way of interacting.

Chapter 6

THE NOT-KNOWING POSTURE: STORIES ABOUT "LEADING FROM BEHIND"

During our long professional education and training it is emphasized that *we* are the experts at identifying, diagnosing, and treating problems—and we are. We do know a great deal about human behaviors and psychopathology, about what's wrong or why something isn't working. We soon come to believe that we are the irrefutable authority and hold ultimate responsibility for a desirable therapeutic outcome. DeJong and Berg (1998) describe this mindset and way of conducting ourselves as a "problem-solving" approach.

Increasingly, both professionals and the public have become dissatisfied with this expert-driven approach, and there is a burgeoning movement to make therapy a client-driven endeavor. This new approach not only is pragmatic but also better fits with the general postmodern view that there is no ultimate truth or right way of doing things. SFBT is one of the first models to insist on taking on this "not-knowing" posture (Anderson & Goolishan, 1992), which recognizes that clients are experts on their own lives and know what will best fit their needs. It is also consistent with the assumption of respecting and accepting client values and beliefs. In clinical practice, this posture makes it possible for the therapist to ask questions rather than telling clients what to do, making pronouncements about what was the matter with their childhood, and telling them what they can do to undo or fix it. It sounds rather simple, but it is so counter to our training and natural compulsion to be helpful to anyone who suffers or is in pain that it is often difficult to put into practice.

UNCONDITIONAL ACCEPTANCE OF CLIENTS' BELIEF AND VALUES

Having respect for clients' right to choose their values and belief systems begins with accepting the religious, spiritual, or ideological beliefs clients bring to the relationship and working within their frame of reference. To learn the client's beliefs and values, ask questions such as, "How do you explain to yourself why you have this kind of problem?" or "Why do you think you are having this problem at this time in your life?" or "What is your understanding of why your son is having so much difficulty in school?"

The thinking behind these questions is our belief that all humans try to organize and explain the events, situations, and problems in their lives—to put them into some coherent order. Ultimately, this way of making sense of the world shapes one's behavior, feelings, and thinking and affects everything one does: where to work, which partner to choose, what to eat, and so on. These beliefs may be idiosyncratic and even exotic at times, but they guide clients' lives in very real ways. Therefore, it makes sense and is efficient and effective to work with the client's belief system rather than trying to change it. To do otherwise is presumptuous—it would be arrogant and wrong to think that our way of organizing the world is superior to that of our clients. Many professionals believe that it is their duty and responsibility to educate their clients and change their views (without the client's request or permission), because they believe that the "incorrect" or "irrational" belief caused the client's problems. This kind of thinking not only makes it difficult to connect with our clients, but also requires much arduous work from the therapist.

COMMUNICATING RESPECT FOR THE CLIENT

A simple question such as "You must have a good reason to . . . (drink a lot, become angry, cut yourself, want to kill yourself, etc.)" can generate an amazing turnaround in clients. Consider the structure of this sentence and notice how it differs from the traditional approach of addressing client's problems: "Why are you drinking so much?" or "Why are you losing your temper?" or "How long have you had your temper?" or "Why do you think you are inferior?" These questions imply that there is something wrong with the client for "losing your temper, drinking too much, or feeling inferior, so let's find out what is wrong with you and then we can fix it."

"You must have a good reason to . . . ?" says immediately to the client: You seem like a reasonable person, so there must be a good reason for you to do such an insensible act like drinking too much or cutting on yourself. Not surprisingly, many clients come up with very reasonable explanations of their intentions. This way of beginning the dialogue establishes a respectful and immediately positive and cooperative relationship between the client and therapist. It positions the client as an expert who narrates the thoughts behind the "bizarre" or "irrational" behavior.

The following short story demonstrates this posture of communicating respect for a junior high school student who came to school in a bizarre outfit. It would be logical to think that the student's outlandish behavior indicated some very serious underlying problem that required immediate intervention.

Good Reason
Contributed by In-Sook Choi, Seoul, Korea

I consult at a junior high school as a mental health counselor. One day I came to work and found an air of quiet agitation and people running around and whispering, which was a contrast to the usual orderly, serene atmosphere of the school. I learned eventually that a male student had come to school without his trousers! All junior high school students in Korea wear uniforms; hat, jacket, trousers, book bags, scarf, even shoes and socks must conform to regulation colors and design. You can imagine the commotion such a dramatic sight as a boy without trousers stirred among faculty and students alike.

Staff immediately decided that the student must have lost his sanity and worried that this must be an indication that he was becoming psychotic. There was talk of calling his parents and then an ambulance to take him to a psychiatric hospital. The only thing that slowed down this process was that nobody knew what the procedure for this was. After realizing that they did not have an official procedure, the principal turned to me and asked me what my opinion was. I wondered aloud if anyone had asked the boy what might be his "good reason" for coming to school wearing only his underwear and jacket. It turned out that nobody had asked the student.

Eventually, a tall, strong male teacher was selected to question the student about his bizarre behavior. The teacher was at a loss as to how to ask the boy and where, and what to do if the boy were to become violent, and so on. With detailed coaching, the male teacher eventually went to the classroom and asked the student to step outside into the hall. In a quiet and gentle voice he asked the boy, "You must have a very good *reason for coming to school without the rest of your uniform today." The boy calmly answered, "Yes, of course I do." The teacher followed this up with "I would like to hear your* good reasons *for coming to school without your complete uniform." It turned out that the student felt that one teacher had reprimanded him unfairly the day before for speaking disrespectfully to the teacher and this was the only way he could think of to protest the teacher's unfair punishment.*

Simply by asking from a position of "You must have a good reason to . . ." the school staff and the principal saved potential embarrassment and perhaps irreparable damage to the student and his family.

The phrase, "leading from one-step behind" was first coined by Cantwell and Holmes (1994) in describing a social constructionistic approach to the hierarchical relationship between a supervisor and trainee or student. Cantwell and Holmes describe the relationship as inevitably and necessarily having a "leading" or teaching component, but done from behind, gently, with questions that raise possibilities and redirect thinking. This concept also applies to therapy. As professionals we offer our special area of expertise and the client acknowledges and pays for this expertise. "Leading from behind" indicates a gentle, respectful approach that recognizes and accepts the client's choice.

Deciding when to lead and when to lag behind requires sensitivity and willingness to allow clients to make informed choices, trusting that they know what is ultimately best for them. Leading from behind begins with listening to what the client says is important, even when it seems to go against common sense and conventional wisdom. Asking questions and listening carefully lead to conversations like this:

> Therapist: (*With genuine curiosity*) So, explain to me again how it is going to be helpful for you to leave the marriage at this stage of your life?
>
> Client: I just think I have to do this right now because I will never know how my life would turn out if I don't do this. Gosh, this is not easy for me to do this, you know.
>
> Therapist: Yes, I can see that this is not an easy decision for you. If it were, you would not be agonizing like this and you would have taken steps already, as many people would have done. So, explain to me again, what are you hoping or expecting to be different for you by leaving the marriage?
>
> Client: I just need to know whether I am doomed to live a life defined by other people or if I can make my own decision and live with the consequences.
>
> Therapist: So you want to know whether you are able to meet the challenges of the unknown and learn to be grown-up enough to accept the consequences of your choice.
>
> Client: Yes, that's exactly what I mean. I have to grow up and if I make a mistake, I have to learn to live with the consequences. It's very scary but I can't live just a straight and narrow life like I have for the last 35 years. I feel like I'm choking with boredom.

Therapist: So suppose you leave your marriage and family, how are you expecting your life to be different?

Client: Well, I will decide what to eat, when to eat, what to do with my time, who to see or not see, what kind of job to have, how many hours to work, and how much money I need to earn, things like that.

Therapist: Suppose you do all those things. What will you be doing then that you are not doing right now?

The therapist's assumption of the client's competency and curiosity led to the client's unexpected search for meaning. At first, the client was unable to articulate her needs; she just wanted to get out of the marriage and, as she described it, the "unhappy, dull pain of being married." By sticking closely to the client's words and recognizing that the goal of leaving the marriage could lead to further disappointment and frustration, the therapist led from one step behind by patiently asking the client to clarify her thoughts. Until these questions were posed to her in a gentle, caring, and not-knowing manner, the client may have thought that the act of leaving itself would solve her pain. However, a few minutes later, the client was able to articulate a very different goal: to be independent and live with the consequences of her own decisions. This approach demands us to listen to our clients in a new way.

Someone Competent is in Charge Here
Contributed by John Briggs, Milwaukee, Wisconsin

Diagnoses and labels can be very destructive when we—clients and therapists included—believe they are written in stone. In truth, these labels can be changed when we allow clients to take charge of defining and accomplishing their own goals, as this story beautifully reveals.

When Jane showed up in my office, she was quite certain she was in the wrong place. She had already canceled one visit with me and made a point of informing me that she'd considered canceling this meeting as well. In fact, she wanted me to know that she was only here due to the persistence of her psychiatrist, who wanted her to try therapy as an adjunct to the medications she was taking for depression and anxiety. Her psychiatrist had worked hard to convince her that this experience would be different from her previous experiences with therapy, but apparently she was not convinced.

Her face was red. I was not sure if that was from anxiety, fear, embarrassment, or a combination. She chose her words very carefully as she explained the "referral." She also put forth quite an effort to make sure I understood that she was not a "self-referral" but was at least willing to give me a chance.

I sincerely thanked her for the opportunity, adding that I valued her expertise on therapy that wasn't helpful and asking for some clues about how I could be helpful. She assertively explained that I should stay awake during our conversations, should not act like I knew all the answers, and should merely listen respectfully and with care. I told her I could probably offer guarantees on the first two and would do my best on the third. I then explained that she may have heard from the psychiatrist that I ask a lot of strange and perhaps dumb questions, but the answers people give to those questions are generally very helpful. Tentatively, but with a kind of curiosity, she granted me permission to proceed.

In the course of our first meeting, she told me about her previous treatments: the therapist who repeatedly fell asleep, the therapist who suggested she should consider a sex-change operation (which she considered), and the numerous hospital admissions that happened with regularity every autumn. After a long consecutive run of annual autumn hospitalizations, Jane came to identify these periods as her "fall episodes." She had nightmares and flashbacks of rape and spent a lot of time alone, avoiding people. She also told me she often thought about killing herself. I was impressed with how much information this woman was able to communicate in a relatively short period of time.

Jane was 50 years old, married, and had impressive support and love from her husband. She was pleased that I was interested in meeting this man who was apparently so wonderful. I think she was pleased that I was more interested in meeting a good, decent human being than I was in "collecting collateral data" on her, as she put it.

Jane had a plethora of health problems, including diabetes, high blood pressure, hypothyroidism, irritable bowel syndrome, obesity, a rectal fissure (resulting from a preadolescent rape), asthma, and sleep apnea. Her gall bladder recently had been removed.

In response to the miracle question, she simply stated, "I would have a will to live and would feel confident that I was going to stay out of the hospital this fall." Earlier in our session, she had indicated that the current combination of medications she was taking (antianxiety and antidepressant) was more helpful than the numerous permutations she had tried in the past. I was curious about this and asked how she was taking advantage of feeling better. She was amused by the question but had ready answers. Specifically, she indicated she was more active, went outdoors more, socialized more, and was better able to see the beauty of the fall season. She scaled her current level at 2 when 10 was her day after the miracle.

In my feedback at the end of our conversation, it was amazingly easy to give a long list of compliments to this seemingly problem-ridden lady. She was the only college-educated member of her family, was well-read, had a marvelously witty sense of humor, was assertive, loved theatre, was compassionate, and was able to see the beauty of the fall season.

I remember being particularly struck by her comment that she liked fall and thought it was a beautiful season despite her numerous "fall episodes." As I went down the list of compliments, it was clear that she was not only surprised but also pleased with her accomplishments and my recognition of them. In closing, I simply asked her to pay attention to the things she liked most about fall and said I hoped she would come back and share her findings with me.

In two weeks she returned with a story about a miserable experience she had the day after our first meeting. She underwent a painful colonoscopy procedure, which she dreaded. The physician was two hours late and had a group of medical students in the examination room with him, which added humiliation to her pain, anxiety, and frustration. There was also an error in her husband's direct deposit, which resulted in several overdrafts at their bank. She indicated that all this pointed to the beginning of her fall episode and said, "I was going to kill myself."

The "was" of this statement seemed amplified somehow, so I asked what happened: "It sounds like this all happened two weeks ago. How did you bounce back so quickly?" She explained that her husband encouraged her to give herself a break—that she had had a rough week and was understandably frustrated and down. This was a normal reaction. She went on to lecture me that these external events, over which she had no control, couldn't possibly be signs of another fall episode, without recognizing that she had just reversed her position.

She used this new perspective as a springboard to observe the positives of fall: cool, fresh air; cool lake breezes; the return of college students to her part of town; the palpable energy that came along with them; going to the theater; new television programming; summer movies available on video; energizing weather; and the coming rejuvenation of nature during winter. After listing autumn's qualities, she exclaimed, "And I signed up for an exercise program!" I was amazed.

During our third meeting, she described her continued successes, boasting that fall was half over and she had stayed out of the hospital. Her confidence about reaching this goal had risen from a 2 to a 5. Of course, I was very impressed with the progress and told her so. She also reported that her sex drive was increasing and that she wanted me to meet her husband and talk about this.

Another fascinating thing occurred in our third meeting. Out of the blue, she asked if I could explain her diagnosis to her. This caught me off guard a bit, so I asked her to clarify the question. She agreed. "My diagnosis is major depression, moderate, recurrent. I am bothered by the recurrent part. This means that I'm never going to get away from this." Not knowing exactly what to do, I pulled out a copy of the DSM-IV, and we discovered together that major depression seems to exist in a continuum that includes mild, moderate, severe, and severe with psychotic features. She was pleased to be labeled at the lower end of the continuum. We also discovered a potential qualifier: the terms "in partial remission" and "in full remission." Upon this discovery, she proudly proclaimed her goal: "I want to be in full remission."

In the fourth and fifth sessions, Jane continued to describe an improved mood, less anxiety, a higher activity level, and an improved relationship with her husband. I was fortunate to meet him and I found him to be very kind, compassionate, and supportive. She was pleased and proud to have me notice. She talked about

occasional setbacks between our meetings and was impressed with
herself for not allowing them to "spiral down and out of control."
We talked about how she was doing this and what she was now
doing differently, and she readily described taking charge of her life
instead of being a pawn to the depression. She said she was taking
better advantage of her medications and supportive husband by in-
creasing her activity level, spending more time outdoors, exercising
more, socializing more, having hope, and taking better care of her
medical problems. She stopped heeding the warnings former ther-
apists and psychiatrists had given her about the inevitability of "re-
current episodes." As she listened to herself talk, she sat up straight
and exclaimed with a hint of defiance, "At least someone compe-
tent is in charge this year!"

Our eighth meeting was on December 23, and I began by com-
plimenting her on achieving her goal. She seemed confused at first,
but I reminded her that the fall season had officially ended and she
had avoided both her fall episode and hospitalization. We spent
the rest of the meeting laughing and bragging about all she had
done instead of having a fall episode, and the list was lengthy and
easy to recall.

Her husband had taken her to a resort over the Thanksgiving
holiday—"much nicer accommodations than the county mental
health complex. Too bad the insurance company won't pay for
that!" She started talking about dreams for herself and her hus-
band during retirement and how she was looking to the future.
They even started looking at retirement properties and log cabins.

Jane is now working on her second consecutive year without a
fall episode, and she doesn't miss it a bit. She continues to have
dreams and hopes for the future, which are only occasionally in-
terrupted by the normal setbacks that occur in most of our lives.

Briggs demonstrated the fact that he was listening for some way
to change Jane's perception of herself as doomed to live out her diagnostic label when he picked up on her use of the past tense: "I
was going to kill myself." His pursuit of this difference marked a
significant turning point in the case. Such subtle shading of a word
here and there can make a world of difference: It did not take a
sledgehammer to drill into Jane's head that she was not doomed
to suffer every fall. All it took was a little tickle with a feather!

A Father's Choice: Leading from Behind
Contributed by Melissa Darmody, Dublin, Ireland

This case, about a man wanting relief from painful memories of an event from the past, is a beautiful example of leading from behind. The therapist in this story strikes a delicate balance by making suggestions about the healing process but still allowing the client to make his own decisions about his course of action.

Connor was an Irish writer in his mid-fifties who sought counseling regarding childhood sexual abuse he had experienced. He was married with three children and described his life as "for the most part" satisfying. However, he wanted to "integrate" some feelings that were "left over from the abuse" in order to have a fuller, happier life. During the first session, he said it was important that he tell me about his past life experiences so that I could understand his current "longing" for resolution.

Connor described growing up in a large family with 10 children. He characterized his parents as loving and good providers, although his father had little input into everyday family life, as it was necessary for him to work long hours in order to provide for such a large family. With his parents busy caring for his younger siblings, Connor remembered learning that it was important to "get on with things" and to "find your own way" in life.

In school, he was very interested in sports and began to excel at soccer as a way to gain recognition. When he was 12 years old, a soccer coach took a special interest in him and began to give him presents and invite him to special events. At first Connor greatly appreciated the attention because his father was not interested in soccer and was unable to spend much time with him. Unfortunately, the coach's attention gradually turned confusing and unpleasant. He began to make sexual advances that were abusive, and Connor was unclear about how to get out of the situation. Looking back, he described himself as an innocent, naive child who found the unwanted affection perplexing. No one in Connor's family seemed to notice his confusion and distress. Because he found it impossible to discuss the abuse with his family, he had to find his own "escape." The Catholic church provided an escape route for Connor. At the age of 16 he entered the clergy.

When Connor entered the clergy, no one in the family asked about his motivation for such a life-changing decision; they accepted his choice without question. Connor subsequently found life in the clergy pleasant but not meaningful. Eventually, he began to question the choice he had made, and, after 30 years of service, he left the clergy to marry and start a family of his own.

Since his childhood, Connor had questioned the events in his life that had lead to the choices he made. Ten years before he came for counseling, he started a journal in an attempt to "figure out some of these events." By now, Connor felt that he had already done quite a lot of work. He had worked through his bitterness towards the Catholic church and had found it helpful to disclose the abuse to his wife and siblings. We discussed some of the aspects of his life that he felt were his strengths, and he pointed out his family, sense of humor, and his feet being firmly planted in reality. Connor felt these qualities were what had allowed him to move on from the abuse.

However, some events were still haunting him and making him question significant events in his life. Connor decided that it was important for him to find a way to "work through" the thoughts and memories that disturbed him, and to find his own way of piecing together the past so that he could deal with it. When asked how he would know that he had "worked through his abuse experience," he explained that he wanted to stop questioning the choices he had made in his life and to release the bitterness that lingered regarding these choices. He had recently enlarged a photograph of himself at the age when the abuse started and was asking questions of his siblings to try to figure things out. Connor was clear that his goal was to move on and start living his life fully. He was also clear that his writing about earlier events was important in order for him to develop a sense of the past and to "integrate" this into his current life.

During the second session we again discussed what he already had been doing that helped him to "integrate and move on." He again described all the creative ways he had done this, including keeping the journal. However, he mentioned that the more he wrote, the more he noticed that there was one thing about the past that he found particularly troubling: the fact that his parents did not stop him or question him about his decision to enter the clergy at such a young age. Connor felt this was uncaring of his parents. Furthermore, now a father himself, Connor felt he would at least discuss such a drastic life choice if any of his children were in a similar situation. Connor found it difficult to accept the fact that his parents had not noticed the abuse he suffered and stopped the relationship with the coach.

Connor said that he had some important questions to ask his father (his mother had died a few years earlier). He needed his father to answer these questions and validate that the abuse took place. He felt that having a discussion with his father would be the first small step toward understanding how this chain of events had been allowed to happen. Unfortunately, he felt unable to ask these questions because his father was elderly and his siblings were afraid that the "news" of Connor's abuse would upset him to the point of risking his health. During this session, we discussed the possibility of writing letters to both his mother and father regarding his feelings and the questions, and then to write a letter to himself imagining what they would say in response. He thought about this and said he might give it a try.

Connor came to the third session very pleased with his progress. He had written a letter to his mother and then written himself an imaginary response from her. This had given him a sense of relief from the blame he had placed on his mother. He had recalled times when his mother warned him to be careful around the coach and now felt that she had tried to protect him in her own way. The letter to his father had not been as useful, and there were still some questions he wanted to discuss in person with him.

Connor explained that he and his father did not have a real relationship. He said his father was like a "news reporter" of the family gossip. Once the family news was reported, there was little else for Connor and his father to discuss. Connor felt that the first small step toward possibly talking about his past with his father would be to improve communication between them. We spent the remainder of the session discussing various ways Connor might be able to change how he and his father were interacting, such as directly asking his father what he thought about certain family gossip, what he guessed other members of the family might do or *think, or what his wife would have said about such an event had she still been living, and, more personally and intimately, asking whether he missed his wife and so on. Connor decided to really listen to his father and talk to him about some things other than family gossip.*

During the fourth session, Connor said that he had been able to change the way he and his father communicated by engaging his father in a more open way. To gain a sense of how close he was to his goal, I asked Connor to place himself on a scale where 10 would be the best it could possibly be with his father and 1 was the worst communication had been. He placed himself at a 4 or 5 and said that a 7 would be good enough. He felt that a 10 would mean talking more openly with his father, not necessarily about the abuse. I asked him what he thought it would take for him to talk to his father a little bit more openly or to ask him directly. Connor agreed that in order to move up on the scale he would need to do more of what he had found helpful since the previous session: listening to his father and reacting to him in a different way.

In the fifth session, Connor said that he had been talking to his father and communication was improving greatly. Although he hadn't brought up the abuse, Connor had found the courage to tell his father that he had been coming to counseling. He said he now felt that his father was sorry "in his own way." His father had suggested that Connor keep a sum of money that Connor had borrowed from him. His father saw this as a form of compensation for the loss of his childhood.

Connor was very pleased with how things were progressing and felt that the improvement in his relationship with his father was allowing him to explore the decisions he had made regarding his life's choices. He had also talked with his siblings about the possibility of telling his father about the abuse, and they were more open to it. I congratulated him and suggested that he continue to do more of the work he was doing, as it seemed to be helpful in his goal of reestablishing a real relationship with his father.

When Connor arrived at the sixth session, he was noticeably calm, relaxed, and full of confidence. I asked him about his good mood, and he replied that he had been able to discuss his concerns

*with his father in a real way and that his father's actions now made
sense. I asked him to explain.*

Connor related that after the last meeting he had gathered the
courage to talk to his father about the abuse. His father had been re-
ceptive and caring. This allowed them to have a very open, honest
conversation about Connor's concerns regarding his father's lack of
guidance and consideration. His father responded by telling Connor
the story of growing up with his own father, who had been an over-
bearing, dictatorial man who controlled everything his children did.
Connor's father had found this behavior oppressive and demanding and had vowed that he would never treat his own children in
this fashion. He prided himself on allowing his children to make
their own decisions and choose their paths in life.

When Connor had decided to enter the clergy his father had
thought that it was his son's decision to make and therefore he had
not wanted to interfere. He had thought he was being the best possible father he could be to Connor. He expressed strongly to Connor
that his lack of interference had not been a sign of indifference, but
the opposite. He had felt at the time that the greatest sign of love
and caring would be to respect the choice that his son had made.

After hearing this, Connor realized that he had mistaken his father's way of caring for indifference. This had released him from
the anger and blame he had been holding toward his father for the
abuse and for his chosen escape from it. The conversation with his
father allowed Connor to discuss his feelings and concerns and put
together the pieces of the puzzle he had always felt were missing.

I asked Connor if he felt he had "integrated" these past events.
He answered that he had and that along the way he had reestab-
lished his relationship with his father in a way that was meaningful for both of them. He said that this was more than he had hoped
for. We laughed together that he had gone beyond the 1-to-10 scale
to a 12, when all he had been expecting was a 7. I spent some time
validating and confirming what Connor identified that he needed
to continue doing to keep things on track. At the end of the session, I congratulated him and wished him well.

In addition to illustrating the not-knowing posture, this case
shows how therapists can work with clients' desire to understand

their past. Darmody did an excellent job of helping Connor find the most useful and helpful way to interpret his past. Without dictating a "proper" course of action, she allowed him to find his own ways of achieving resolution. That Connor chose to begin making sense of his past by changing the way he was living in the present is to the credit of both him and the therapist. Unquestionably, his new understanding of the past will positively affect how he lives his future.

Mr. Wang's Spirit World: SFBT in Cross-Culture Cases
Contributed by Insoo Kim Berg, Milwaukee, Wisconsin

Frequently we are asked about how the SFBT approach works in cases involving different cultures. Regardless of the problem or the demographics of the client population, SFBT therapists not only respect and value clients' perceptions and ideas but also actively incorporate them into the therapy process. This is because SFBT techniques are designed to empower clients to determine the course and direction of therapy, and treatment goals are based upon what clients want to have happen in their lives. We think this is well conveyed through this story.

While I was teaching in Hong Kong, a social worker requested a consultation with me, explaining that the Wang family case had been referred to the counseling agency where she was working because of the dire needs of the two young children. The social worker felt at a loss as to how to help Mr. Wang, who had been her client for three years since Mrs. Wang abandoned the family. In the middle of an elaborate birthday party she had organized in a fancy restaurant, Mr. Wang's wife left the room full of their family and friends to take a call on her cell phone. When she returned, she told him that she was leaving him for another man and abruptly left the party. She never contacted him again. Mr. Wang soon quit his job as a policeman to take care of his two children. I agreed to interview Mr. Wang along with the social worker who had requested the consultation.

Since that time he had been dogged by a severe depression and had been painfully ruminating about his fate, to the extent that he had to be hospitalized. On one occasion, he called a psychiatric emergency service from the rooftop of a 14-story building, where he was threatening to jump. He had subsequently received numerous treatments at psychiatric facilities, been prescribed a variety of medications for his bouts of depression, and endured many psychological evaluations, all to no avail. He still suffered from depression, slept excessively, and stayed in bed all day. Consequently, he had failed at times to feed the children and take them to day-care and kindergarten. A homemaker service had then been offered and protective services were brought in to secure services for the children's welfare. These interventions seemed to have little effect on Mr. Wang, who still talked of suicide now and then and refused to take medications prescribed by various psychiatrists.

Mr. Wang quarreled with his family and his in-laws and even lost contact with his network of friends and neighbors. Because of his reduced income on public assistance, he could not afford his apartment and was forced to move into a public housing project. This further contributed to his sense of failure and perpetuated his self-criticism and remorse. He gained weight and complained of a lack of energy. The social worker was overwhelmed with this case and deeply concerned about Mr. Wang's periodic talk of hopelessness and suicide.

A dour-looking man in his early thirties, Mr. Wang appeared pudgy and puffy, as if he had just gotten out of bed for our 2 P.M. appointment. Barely managing to crack a smile, he answered most of my questions in Cantonese, although he clearly understood the English I was using. When I asked Mr. Wang why he imagined he was suffering such misfortune for such a long time, he said he believed that it was the result of a curse perpetrated on him by an element from the spirit world. I then asked him how he thought this curse had fallen on him, whereupon he explained that this particular type of spirit world (which is worshipped in Taiwan) is known to be vengeful when people have not respected its teaching. Mr. Wang said that he had tried to follow its teaching for the past 20 years and had tried to be good to others. However, he had made one mistake—he had burned the sacred altarpiece that he kept in his apartment. He had done this at the insistence of his wife, who was not interested in learning or obeying the teaching of the spirit world. Mr. Wang believed that he was being punished for having burned the altarpiece; however, he also thought the spirit world understood that he had been forced to burn it against his wishes.

Recognizing that he had studied the inner workings of this spirit world for close to 20 years, I asked him a scaling question: Assuming that 10 meant that he had been sufficiently punished for burning the altarpiece (at which point the spirit world would stop punishing him) and 1 stood for the heaviest punishment the spirit world decided he deserved to suffer, where would he stand on the scale? Without hesitation, Mr. Wang answered that now—three years after the heaviest punishment, his wife's leaving, was leveled—he thought he was at a 7.

> *Therapist: So, it took three years to go from 1 to 7. Where did you get such patience and persistence to hang in there all this time?*
>
> *Mr. Wang: (With downcast eyes) I have two young children who need me and I have to hang in there. I worry about them because they don't have their mother as they should have.*
>
> *Therapist: So, you love your children very much and it sounds like you worry about them a lot.*
>
> *Mr. Wang: (With a sigh) Yes, I do. I worry about them all the time because they are so young and they need their mother.*
>
> *Therapist: So, how did you manage to hang in there for three years? It's a long time to suffer. I can imagine many fathers in your situation would have either abandoned the children and run away from the responsibility or started drinking a long time ago. I wonder how you manage to hang in there without abandoning your children?*
>
> *Mr. Wang: (With slight indignation) I could never do that to my kids. I'm not that kind of person. I always tried to help others and to live right.*
>
> *Therapist: I'm sure you have. Considering how terrible you must have felt three years ago when all this began, how in the world did you manage to get all the way up to 7?*

> Mr. Wang: (With a little more force) *I keep thinking about my children needing me and how they don't have anybody to look after them.*
>
> Therapist: *You are right about that—that they need you. So, let me ask you a slightly different kind of question this time. How much more time will it take you to get from 7 to 10?*
>
> Mr. Wang: (Thoughtfully) *I would say about another year, at most, a year and a half.*
>
> Therapist: *Wow, that's not much—I mean the time. I'm sure you can handle that considering how difficult it must have been when the problem first began three years ago.*
>
> Mr. Wang: *I think it will be easier to get from 7 to 10 than to go from 1 to 7.*
>
> Therapist: *That's an interesting way of looking at it. How do you explain to yourself the fact that it will be easier to go from 7 to 10 than it was to go from 1 to 7?*
>
> Mr. Wang: *Because I have shown the spirit world that I am not going to give up on my children and that it should know by now that I am a good person and that I tried to do good things in my life whenever I could.*
>
> Therapist: *So what do you have to do during the next year and a half while you are waiting to get from 7 to 10?*
>
> Mr. Wang: (With a little more energy) *I just have to remain steady and stable.*
>
> Therapist: *So, how confident are you that you will remain steady and stable in the next year or so?*
>
> Mr. Wang: *I am very confident that I can do it because I feel like the worst is over for me.*

I asked Mr. Wang what else he was doing while he waited patiently for the time to pass. He related that, at the urging of the social worker, he had started going to church because he realized he needed to expand his social life and learn about raising little girls. At this point, we took a 15-minute break in the session.

I consulted with a team of the counseling staff and then offered the following feedback: "Mr. Wang, I speak for everybody on the *team when I express our admiration for your single-minded goal of wanting to raise your daughters right. It would have been easy for you to abandon your children, and we imagine that many men in your situation would have started drinking or gambling" (both of which are serious problems for men in Hong Kong). Mr. Wang agreed and interjected that he began drinking a little but decided it was not good for him. I responded, "But you have been very clear that your first responsibility was to raise your daughters, especially because they need their mother, and you have really tried to be both mother and father to them. It took a great deal of strength to have gone all the way up to 7 from 1 and it shows how determined you are to remain true to yourself in spite of a tragedy that not many people suffer. You remained true to your beliefs, which is truly impressive. We agree with you that your problem seems to be in a transitional state—that is, it is on the way to being over, and the important thing is to remain patient and stable. You know exactly what you need to do and you already know how to remain stable and patient because you have three years of experience already. The only suggestion we can offer you at this time is to keep doing it, including your joining the church and expanding your social network. Clearly, you need to keep your faith and continue to be a good father to your children. I am sure your children will realize someday how much you love them and how much you have sacrificed for them."*

As we were winding down the interview, Mr. Wang finally spoke English as he thanked me, and he had a broad smile on his face.

A year after this interview I made a return visit to Hong Kong and met the social worker who brought Mr. Wang for consultation. She reported that Mr. Wang is doing quite well and his scale of finishing his ordeal has reached 9 and that he now jokes about how he will not take his wife back.

We are often asked whether SFBT works with "ethnic minority clients" and how therapists can work with clients whose cultural and ethnic backgrounds differ from their own. I believe this kind of question comes from the assumption that the therapist must carry the burden of being the expert who knows everything there is to know about the problem (DeJong & Berg, 1998), including whether their religious beliefs make sense. Mr. Wang's interview nicely demonstrates that, contrary to this assumption, the client has the answer to his dilemma. He knew exactly what it would take for him to successfully wait out the remaining time of the punishment he had to endure. I did not need to know everything about the spirit world that Mr. Wang believed in, but I did need to know that it was important to him.

It was not my job to decide whether Mr. Wang's beliefs made sense or not. What was significant was that they made sense to him, a reasonable man with a clear sense of what was important to him: raising his two young daughters in the absence of their mother. It is amazing that Mr. Wang had no difficulty coming up with his own assessment that he was at a 7 out of a possible 10 in the future, when the punishment from the spirit world would be over. He even knew what he needed to do to cope until the time came. No one else could have come up with such sensible and fitting solutions.

Until the therapist made a point of asking questions that solicited his ideas for solution, that is, until he was put in the position of having to provide certain information, Mr. Wang might not have known that he was so close to finishing up his penitence or that he needed to be steady and patient until it was over. It is also probable that he was not aware of what he had already done, such as joining a church group for the purpose of expanding his social contacts and making new friends.

Staying Sick and Staying Married: Working With Victims of Domestic Abuse
Contributed by Baruch Shulem, Jerusalem, Israel

Sometimes accepting the client's wishes can be a challenge, especially in cases involving domestic violence. However, despite a therapist's best intentions, simply urging victims to leave violent relationships when they are not willing or don't feel able to leave does little to mitigate the dangerous—sometimes even potentially lethal—situations that imprison them. If a client feels unable or unwilling to follow her therapist's advice and leave an abusive relationship, she may feel judged and criticized, which further contributes to the perception of helplessness and inadequacy that so often paralyzes victims of ongoing domestic abuse. Typically, in order to empower victims of domestic violence, a therapist must be not only skilled and compassionate, but also infinitely patient and respectful, as Shulem is in this case.

Samantha, a 55-year-old married mother of 12, came to therapy because of her husband's ongoing violence. She had been in therapy on and off for years, and came in this time "as usual" when she was unable to continue to function and keep up a good front. Her husband was well known in the legal community as an excellent lawyer. Over the years, he had always refused to come in for therapy, saying that psychology was useless, that they could take care of the problem themselves, and that his wife alone was to blame for the problem they had in the marriage. Not surprisingly, he refused to come in this time as well.

Samantha's husband started behaving violently toward her the first week of their marriage, when they had a small misunderstanding. Samantha was totally unprepared for this and blamed herself for the problem. She felt ashamed and feared "going public" about what had happened. So she learned quickly to obey her husband and keep the peace. Her husband's violence continued with a frequency of about three times a month. Samantha's injuries had never required that she be hospitalized, but she had received medical treatment a number of times. She had two requirements that pertained both to herself and to therapy: She would keep the abuse a secret, and there could be no talk about divorce. Samantha explained that the taboos around abuse and divorce were culturally, religiously so strong in her community that there was no room for discussion, because the children belonged to their father in case of a divorce. In addition, even if she got the legal custody of the children, there would be very little means for her to force her powerful husband to support the children financially in the manner that they deserved.

I accepted the two rules. I then started by asking about the times when things were a little better. Samantha quickly answered that when she was unable to function her husband stopped behaving violently and became helpful and even supportive. The cycle was paradoxical: She became overwhelmed and he became helpful.

Then she would go to therapy and "get better," and the tension would start rising until her husband was violent again.

I explored with Samantha how her being "unable" helped the couple's relationship but was at the expense of her children. She said that she had never thought of her "weakness" as being helpful to her relationship with her husband. She didn't like being weak and wanted to take care of her children. Being weak precluded caring for the children, although it helped her relationship with her husband.

When I asked Samantha to imagine a miracle in which the problem was solved, she said that after the miracle she would have a supportive husband and she could continue to care productively for the children. I explored with Samantha how she might find a way to be both weak in relation to her husband and yet strong enough to care for her children, but she had no idea how she might do this. So at the end of the session, I suggested that for homework she should notice if there were any times when this or something like this happened.

The following week, Samantha returned and said she didn't have any ideas about the homework. However, she did report that some years ago she had, in a moment of great weakness, told her husband that she might commit suicide. She was crying and very emotional when she told him this. Her husband had become very frightened, and they had their first "honeymoon" period without violence. She had even been able to care for the children during this time, which had lasted for two lovely weeks.

I asked Samantha, "How might you communicate 'weakness' to your husband while continuing to care for the children?" We talked about how therapy could be used positively as a crutch. The message about her weakness would have to be communicated with a aura of pain and mystery, with the sense that she had reached the end of her rope and the doctor couldn't help. Furthermore, it was important that she not elaborate on the message to her husband, who typically interrogated her about therapy. Samantha would give this explanation to her husband: "The doctor wants to explore the possibility of hospitalization because he is concerned that I am internally sick and only pretending to function in a healthy, happy way. The doctor is greatly concerned about my mental *health, but because I refuse to take medication, he does not think therapy would be of any help. My hidden internal state puts me in jeopardy." Samantha smiled and said she thought the description was actually pretty accurate.*

Three follow-up phone calls in which I asked scaling questions indicated that Samantha had experienced major positive changes in her relationships with both her husband and her children. After a year the improvements remained consistent. I have since seen Samantha at social functions, and she tells me that things are going well because "I stay sick."

At first glance this case seems unusual. However, many women are in similar situations: They don't want to end the marriage; they just want the violence to stop. It would have been very easy for the therapist to disagree with the client's goal of staying married to a violent man, or for the therapist to refuse to work under conditions that constrain the therapeutic options. However, in recognizing and accepting Samantha's wish to not discuss the topic of divorce, the therapist wisely turns over the role of finding a solution to the client, thereby uncovering an exception from long ago. By staying "sick," the wife controls and manages the husband, achieving her goal of staying married and taking care of her children. Thus, she finds a very clever and powerful means of achieving her goal of staying safe. Shulem wisely and skillfully recognized the necessity of respecting Samantha's goal and in doing so empowered her to gain more control over her situation.

It is likely that Samantha's husband never treated her with respect. The immediate and undeniable respect she received from her therapist, who listened carefully to her goals and placed *her* (rather than himself) as the expert in finding a solution, possibly fostered a growing recognition that she had the ability to believe in herself and an inalienable right to be treated with dignity by *everyone* in her life. It's possible that Samantha's growing recognition of her own self-worth may eventually result in a decision to leave her marriage and create a new life for herself, and perhaps not.

This case reminds me of my earliest experience as a foreign student in the late fifties in an American university. I was very naïve, inexperienced in worldly things, and very unfamiliar with the American culture. However, I was surprised to hear very thoughtful American professors, friends, and neighbors talk about how Asian women were treated as inferior, second-class citizens in Asia. One fellow student even volunteered her observation that Asian wives walk three paces behind their husbands—certainly a sign that Asian women accepted this second-class status without complaining. I was very confused and surprised by this observation, because I knew that it was because the wife can tell her husband which way to go! In my family women were strong, tough, and made all the important decisions. I was convinced that most Westerners only looked at the surface and assumed that was how things really were. I knew how wrong such assumptions could be.

This case reminds me of a common saying: "What you see is *not* what you get." That is, how things look on the surface is not how things really are. It seems contradictory, but the therapist and Samantha recognized, without speaking about it, that by pretending to be ill when she was not really ill, Samantha could be in control of her husband, who seemed so powerful, yet so powerless when he believed that he might lose her either by suicide or by an illness. By staying weak, Samantha stayed strong, while her husband stayed really weak because he pretended to be strong. At some unspoken level both Samantha and her husband knew this, and the therapist knew this, too.

If we had read this case 20 years ago when we were less experienced and more naïve about the complexities of the human heart and the infinite number of seeming contradictions inherent in the human condition, we probably would have been indignant. "Why didn't the therapist argue with Samantha? Why didn't he aggressively try to get her to gather up her kids and walk away from her abusive husband?" The answer is: Because it hadn't worked for her in the past, and it undoubtedly wouldn't work now. While telling someone to leave an abusive situation is a response forged out of compassion and concern, if it doesn't fit into the client's beliefs and real-life goals, it not only will fail to help but also may actually make things worse.

Chapter 7

"DO SOMETHING DIFFERENT": INVITING CLIENTS TO DISCOVER UNIQUE SOLUTIONS

The three simple principles of SFBT can be summarized as the following:

1. If it is not broken, don't fix it.
2. If it worked once, do it again.
3. If it doesn't work, don't do it again. Do something different.

So far we have spoken a great deal about the first two rules: By finding out what the client wants, we do not unwittingly tamper with something that the client considers working. This first rule also implies that whatever the client and/or therapist is doing that works should be acknowledged and become the foundation for further solutions. Thus, doing more of what works becomes the solution. The second rule, of course, addresses exception to problems, no matter how small. The task for the client and therapist is to find ways to increase exceptions until the client achieves his or her desired change.

In some situations and occasions it is clear to both the client and therapist that the client needs to do something entirely different from what he or she has been doing to solve problems. How can anyone tell that this point has been reached? Common descriptions of such frustrating situations are: "I feel like I'm hitting a brick wall," "I am saying the same thing over and over until I'm blue in the face," "I feel like I'm spinning my wheels," "I am so tired of yelling and screaming and it can't go on any longer." Indeed, clients seem to have tried everything a reasonable person would try. They have carried out the good old maxim of "If you don't succeed, try, try, again" to an exhausting limit without getting any results. A careful study of such complaints shows that clients are repeating the same unsuccessful solutions and getting the same frustrating results.

These situations call for pattern interruption, that is, making small changes in the familiar action-reaction pattern. Inserting an entirely unexpected element into the pattern can create a totally new pattern. As in computer programming, a small variation in the pattern of human interaction can lead to a very different path. The destination can be surprisingly fun and totally unexpected, as the following cases illustrate.

The beauty of inviting clients to discover their own solutions is that they generate many more unique, creative, and customized solutions than a single therapist ever could.

Too Many Poops in the Pants
Contributed by Harry Korman, M.D., Malmo, Sweden

John's parents, Anna and Magnus, brought him to see me because his "pooping" in his pants was really getting to them. John was five years old and had pooped in his pants all his life. Anna and Magnus were artists, and though they were both successful, the beginning of their careers had been tough, as most artists' careers are. John was their first child, and they both took their parenting very seriously. They read as much as they could to learn about encopresis and, of course, they tried to train John in the most proper manner they knew.

When I asked about exceptions, Anna and Magnus said that the only time they could remember John not pooping in his pants was a couple of months ago when he visited his grandparents for a week. When I asked John why he used his grandparents' potty instead of pooping in his pants, he answered with a long-winded and complicated story about swimming and water, which left me totally confused. Anna and Magnus mentioned that the pooping didn't really seem to be a problem for John himself, and I tended to agree.

Anna's attitude was that John would grow out of it. She did not seem very worried. Magnus, on the other hand, expressed an intense reaction to the situation. Although he was not terribly bothered by the pooping itself, which occurred several times a day, he was distressed by the fact that it was becoming increasingly difficult for him to touch the child. He explained, "He always smells of feces, and I find myself holding him at arm's length, not able to hug him close. I don't want to feel disgust toward my own son, and I don't want to feel so irritated by him. This makes me feel terrible about myself and worried about him."

We all agreed that this was indeed a serious problem. Their consultation with the pediatrician ruled out an organic cause. Now they were consulting me because they thought they might need to work through the details of their own childhood, which they worried was the underlying reason for their son's refusal to use the potty.

I asked Anna and Magnus the miracle question. Their answer was that John would tell his parents when he needed to go to the bathroom. The first sign would be that he would tell them immediately after he pooped in his pants instead of walking around smelling bad until they checked him. Magnus thought this would help him feel better about the whole issue and be less irritated by John. Thus, the time they spent together would be more enjoyable for all three of them. I then asked what they had already done to try to solve the problem. It appeared that they had done everything any sensible and reasonable parent would do in such a situation. They had sought advice and followed a number of different and sometimes conflicting suggestions from their family, friends, and professionals, all to no avail. "We tried everything," they said. "Something just must be seriously wrong," muttered Magnus. Anna lifted her eyebrows and appeared to be seriously thinking about her husband's strong reaction to John. I didn't know what to think.

I ended the first session by giving Anna and Magnus many compliments. I was impressed by how responsible and thoughtful they were as parents. I told them that this was indeed a serious problem, not in itself but rather because of that pattern that had developed around it. Both parents nodded in agreement. I continued by explaining how impressed I was by how alert, curious, imaginative, and happy John was, and how well behaved he had been during the session while the adults had talked about his problem. Obviously, Anna and Magnus had done a good job with John in spite of such a vexing problem.

Since they had already tried everything that sensible people would do, my suggestion was to try an experiment: Between now and the next session, Anna and Magnus would do something quite different from what they had already tried, something they had never done before. It should be something that John would never expect them to do and would surprise him, the crazier the better. Their job was to pay attention to how John responded.

At the next session, the parents reported on what had happened: The day after the previous session, they had put John on the potty. Both parents undressed and went stark naked into the bathroom. They both sat down on the edge of the bathtub and said, "cock-a-doodle-doo" several times. Then they left the room without saying anything else.

John was very surprised and kept asking during the following week if this had really happened. The parents neither affirmed nor denied what had happened—they simply changed the subject. John started telling them when he had pooped in his pants, and on two occasions, he even told them that he needed to go potty. In addition, Anna put some water in his potty and had a small boat floating in it. Now the goal was to sink the boat.

Amazed, I asked John, "How did you do it?"

He answered, "I just sit on the potty and then I jiggle my legs and then it comes."

"Is it difficult?" I asked.

He responded, "No."

"What do your Mom and Dad say about this?"

"They are glad," John replied.

"It makes an enormous difference," said Magnus. "I can touch him again. I can hold him close. He still smells sometimes like before, but I am not so irritated and upset about it. And we have this dance, too." Anna looked a little embarrassed as John jumped to his feet shouting, "Come on, daddy!"

Magnus stood up and they both started dancing, lifting their legs high and stomping hard on the floor. They made so much commotion that the whole room shook. With a serious tone of voice they recited, "Poop in the pot, poop in the pot." John laughed and fell to the floor. Magnus hugged his son while Anna and I laughed and laughed. No further sessions were needed. This is an example of a simple solution to a complex and potentially serious problem in the making.

While Korman describes this as a "simple" solution, his intervention is elegant and sophisticated. In a single session, he beautifully emphasized the exceptions that would support the family's ability to develop a successful solution. While taking the parents' concerns seriously and respectfully, Korman pointed out several signs that they were already doing a good job with their son: John was alert, happy, and well behaved throughout the session. He used the miracle question to help Anna and Magnus identify their goals. By suggesting that they do an "experiment," Korman gave the parents freedom to create a new solution.

Shoes Laced Together:
Working with Clients in a Psychotic State
Contributed by Bernie Carter, San Francisco, California

Even the most disturbed patients often come up with solutions that may sound irrational or absurd but in fact are ingenious. When clients with a long psychiatric history are viewed as competent enough to come up with ideas that work for them, they seem to rise to the occasion. It is our experience that even clients with heavy-duty diagnoses frequently have ideas about what might be helpful for them. Listening to these irrational ideas seems to help.

In 1973, I was in my first year of graduate school in clinical psychology. To earn money and gain hours towards licensure, I had taken a position as a resident counselor in a halfway house for people who had been labeled schizophrenic. One of my duties was to distribute prescribed medication to the residents. On this particular night, all the 15 residents except one, who was taking a shower, had received their medication. I completed the charting for the day while I waited for the last resident to come for his medication.

Suddenly he came running into my office, screaming hysterically, "They are trying to crawl inside of me. I want them to leave me alone!" I turned around in my chair and saw the resident standing there naked and dripping wet. He was hopping and spinning around while trying to cover his genitals.

My immediate reaction was fear. I didn't know what to do. I had no training or experience with this sort of acute panic attack, and had only been working on the job for a few weeks. Then I remembered that the resident had seemed untroubled just a few hours ago at dinner. So I asked, "What made you safe at dinner?"

"I had my clothes on," was the reply. The resident seemed less upset while thinking about the question.

So I asked, "Would it help if you put your clothes on?"

This unfortunately seemed to intensify the resident's panic: "No! They are already on my skin! My clothes can't protect me when they are already on my skin."

I knew of no intervention. Later I was told that I "should have confronted the resident about his paranoid delusion" (in hindsight, my guess is that this would have intensified the panic and led to hospitalization). For a few minutes I was as helpless as the resident. Finally, out of desperation I asked, "Has anything helped in the past when your clothes were off?"

The resident's panic seemed to increase as he hopped and spun around the room while screaming at me to do something. Then, suddenly, he stopped and answered my question: "Once I tied my shoes together by their laces. That kept them out." We both looked down, and I saw a pair of gym shoes on the resident's feet. They were unlaced and still wet from the shower. Immediately the resident bent over and quickly tied the laces together. He then stood up, smiling and giggling. His final and triumphant words before hopping back to his shower were, "That should keep them out."

Five minutes later, now wrapped securely in towels, the resident hopped back into my office to receive his medication. Then he hopped off to bed to enjoy an uneventful night's sleep, wearing the shoes. I, on the other hand, was awake for much of the night worried that the resident might experience another panic attack. For the next few days the resident kept his shoes laced closely together and hopped around the halfway house doing chores and helping with meals in an otherwise appropriate manner. No further panic attacks were reported.

The resident's solution was ingenious and worked remarkably well. I would never have thought of that solution. I have to chuckle at the irony that for 25 years afterwards I insisted (with limited success) on trying to provide solutions for my clients, when I had such a good early learning experience that the client holds the solution.

I (IKB) could not help laughing when I pictured this scene involving two very frightened people: a young and inexperienced staff member and a resident with a heavy diagnosis and lots of experience with his mental illness. I immediately realized how clever and ingenious they both were to come up with such a quick and workable solution. Carter, recognizing his own lack of knowledge and skills, turned the problem over to the client—even though he was in the midst of a panic attack—and decided to elicit the client's help in finding a solution. Rather than protest this strange turn of events, the client understood the question and recalled how he successfully overcame the problem in the past.

Other staff members had advised Carter that confronting the resident would have been the most logical and sensible thing to do; however, by doing something different and thinking out of the box, both Carter and the resident came up with a solution far more creative than we would ever find in a textbook. This one event is certainly not the solution to the client's long-standing problem, but it shows a glimpse of what is possible when we look for alternatives to a tried-and-true method.

This case is a great example of the SFBT maxim that the solution does not necessarily have to be related to the problem to be effective.

DEALING WITH ISSUES OF LOSS AND GRIEF

In our training sessions, consultation, and teaching, we are often asked about how SFBT deals with issues of loss and grief. We believe that this kind of question implies that coping with the loss of a significant person is somehow an abnormal state—that one needs to "work through" the grief and that doing this will help put one's life "back on track." It is further implied that there are proper and improper ways of dealing with the grief. We believe this is a limited, misleading way of looking at this serious issue. Loss of any kind—whether it is a significant person, a limb, vigor, or anything else—alters one's life forever. Moving on with one's life means accepting a different life, in many significant and minor ways. Sometimes an individual's personal meaning of life changes forever.

SFBT therapists deal with issues of grief and loss the same way we deal with any other life issue. First, we find out how long ago the loss occurred. If the loss is recent, a crisis approach might be useful: help clients slow down and change gears, take time to be sad, and withdraw from the world for a while. Normalize their response as appropriate and even healthy and suggest that they take time to immerse themselves in the loss. You can also inform them that it takes a considerable amount of time to grieve, and, in fact, the length of the grieving period may indicate how important and meaningful the relationship was. You may suggest that they take some time to think about what aspect of their life with the deceased person they might want to have continued, such as how they enjoyed camping or worked hard to accomplish a dream together, how they consoled each other when needed, or how they prayed together. This is a nice way to show clients that the deceased person's life may not need to be deleted from their own. In the meantime, suggest that the client think about other ways of keeping alive the memory of the deceased.

Coping questions are another nice tool to use when the after-effects of loss are significantly affecting the client's present life. Rather than trying to move clients from one place to another in the grieving process, try to understand what helps keep them going long after the event. How did she discover that keeping the shade drawn and the room dark was helpful? What did he find helpful about staying indoors all the time?

Sometimes clients find it helpful to create or perform a ritual to put the loss behind them, as the family in the following story did. As you will see, each member of the family uniquely adapted the ritual to suit his or her needs.

Bunny Funeral
Contributed by Robin McCarthy, Portland, Maine

The Smiths, a family of four, came to see me soon after their house burned down. Each member of the family had been traumatized in different ways and had different symptoms, such as ruminating about the event, listlessness, sleep disturbance, fear of the stove or any other form of burning fire, extreme sensitivity to the smell of smoke, and acute sensitivity even to someone smoking. Some solutions, such as sharing fears among the family members, recognition that the fire was not anyone's fault and was caused by a mechanical failure, and continued support and reassurance helped to a point, but unfortunately nothing seemed to touch or relieve the lingering sadness the family felt for several months after the fire. They wanted to rebuild their house, but just could not find the energy or enthusiasm for the project after their terrible loss.

The members of the family had safely escaped the exploding and burning house, but their beloved pet rabbit had perished. Listening to their repeated discussions about the rabbit, I recognized the significance of the rabbit's death in the fire and I wondered about the "bunny funeral." Of course, I didn't know what a bunny funeral looked like, but I figured that, like most effective solutions, it would evolve into the shape it was supposed to take.

The family decided the funeral would take place in back of the burned foundation of their house. I asked each family member to consider bringing something meaningful to the funeral. Sarah, the mother, said she would bring carrots. Tom, the father, wanted to bring straw bedding. Ruthie, the older daughter, said she would write a song for the rabbit and sing it at the funeral. After much deliberation, Sally, the younger daughter, had the most curious idea: she decided to bring some math problems.

I showed up for the funeral as planned. It was a Sunday and a snowstorm had descended upon the area. We trudged our way up the hill overlooking their burned-out shell of a house. I carried flowers. The service began with Sarah offering her carrots and Tom offering his straw bedding. Next, Ruthie sang the song she had written for the bunny. Last, Sally offered her math problems. There was not a dry eye to be found at the ceremony!

Something shifted after the funeral. The family decided to start rebuilding their house and to make changes that would help them get on with their lives. These included Tom's decision to pursue an insurance settlement, contacting contractors for the rebuilding, and involving the family on the design of the new house. Sarah also decided on a garden design and chose many items for the new house. They reported that the bunny funeral had allowed them to grieve their losses from the fire in a way that they previously had been unable to do. I was honored to have been a part of it.

One of the things we especially like about this case is how the therapist allowed the family to determine the details of this ritual as well as make their own meaning of the experience. The family members' ideas about appropriate gifts for the rabbit are quite touching. Sally's decision to offer her math problems is a wonderful example of the unpredictability that often characterizes the solutions that families and individuals create when they are offered the support, therapeutic social structure, and freedom to do so. It is as if Sally is keeping the rabbit very much a part of her current daily life.

We like how McCarthy chose to do something different when she realized that discussing the fire and its aftermath was not helping and that some sort of action might be useful. This willingness to consider new options requires humility and an admission of not knowing what to do from the therapist. We can all easily come up with numerous case examples where a therapist's persistence and rigidity hindered the client's case.

Sometimes action speaks louder than words not only to other people but also to us. Cultural and spiritual rituals cannot be overstated as they address both the spoken and unspoken aspects of our relationships in meaningful ways.

Chapter 8

EVEN A LITTLE BIT: STORIES ABOUT SMALL CHANGES

In the late '60s and '70s, I (IKB) worked in a very traditional agency, where intake work was considered separate from therapeutic treatment. One person was in charge of gathering information about the client's history, the presenting symptoms, and the origins of the problem, and another was responsible for the "real" work of treatment. Treatment took a long time because it was believed that a "problem took a long time to develop; therefore, a long, arduous, corrective experience was needed to solve it." (This view is still common among therapists and clients alike. No wonder they are reluctant to begin such an arduous, perilous journey that drains their energy, time, and, of course, their financial resources!)

After the "intake" information was completed, the case was placed in a special basket where any therapist with an opening in his or her schedules would pick it up. All the therapists on staff were oriented toward building long-term relationships with clients, since it was believed that "real therapy" took a long time, perhaps many years. Cases with "involuntary" clients or those involving complicated or chronic problems would sit in the basket for weeks or months at a time, and the list would become quite long.

Therapists were reluctant to get "stuck with" such chronic, hopeless cases and consequently avoided them.

Already developing a taste and some skill for brief therapy, I was the only person on the staff who would rummage through the waiting lists and then go through these cases rather rapidly. I began to develop a small name for myself among the staff as someone who was not afraid of these "difficult, multiproblem cases." My experiences with these cases were quite the opposite of what the rest of the staff expected. I realized that all it takes is a small change—a small shift of posture or slight change of thinking—to make a big difference. This shift of thinking is made possible by our view of clients as having abilities rather than disabilities, as desiring a better life rather than being resistant to change, and as being willing to cooperate rather than set on sabotaging their own interests, as some therapists speculated.

The smaller, simpler, and more immediate the change the client can make, the better. For example, I remember a participant in a training session who was upset and frustrated with a young mother who fed her four young children doughnuts for breakfast. We were struggling with how we could possibly give this mother the nutritional education she needed to prompt her to feed her children cornflakes or hot oatmeal. We were approaching the situation from a problem-solving way of thinking. Indeed, from this perspective, it would be a daunting task to figure out how to teach this young mother who was so uninformed about the children's nutritional needs, in addition to being overwhelmed with life's problems. But it occurred to me that the fact that this young mother at least knew to feed her children *something* in the morning was a good start. The next small task would be to help her supplement doughnuts with cornflakes. Who knows where this small change might lead?

The same type of approach is illustrated by a story once told us by Marika Moisseeff, a rare combination of anthropologist and psychiatrist who works in Paris, France. Moisseeff attended a conference once where the speaker, Aline Vecchiali-Roux, walked to the podium and said, "Alcoholism is a scourge." Then she told the following tale: A man had a terrible drinking problem. He worked as a laborer in a foundry, and he liked to drink beer during his breaks. Unfortunately, he often drank so much that by afternoon he could not keep up with his work. This was a problem not only because he needed his job to support his family, but also because foundry work can be dangerous. Sooner or later, he might have a serious accident and hurt himself or another person.

The man was not interested in giving up drinking, as it was an integral part of his life—something he did with his coworkers, something that made the awful heat of the foundry and the hard physical labor more bearable. The men who worked in the foundry worked hard and drank hard, and that was the way it was. To give up drinking would mean to lose one of life's daily pleasures.

However, he had a good friend who saw him daily because he worked at a stone yard across the street from the foundry. He often had heard the man grumbling because his paycheck was low—a result of not getting his work done or not showing up at all. One day the man was complaining to his friend again about not having enough money. He told him, "I know I drink too much, but I don't want to quit."

The friend didn't answer right away. He did not want to insult the man by offering him advice, but he was concerned because he could see that the drinking was taking its toll physically as well as financially. After sitting quietly for a few moments, the friend said, "I'll tell you what to do and it will make a difference: See those little pebbles over there? Tomorrow before you open a bottle of beer, I want you to pick up one of those pebbles and wash it off so it's nice and clean. When you open a bottle of beer, put the pebble inside the bottle and drink it. When you finish the first bottle with a pebble inside, save the small pebble until the next day. On the second day, you wash another pebble and now you have two pebbles to put into the beer bottle before you drink the beer. Each day thereafter you keep adding one more pebble into the bottle." The man agreed to follow through with what seemed to be a harmless little game and he subsequently got his drinking under control.

Mal's Story: SFBT with Terminally Ill Clients
Contributed by Dorothy (Dotty) Decker, M.S.W., D.C.S.W., L.M.F.T., Plymouth, Michigan

Small change can radically transform the tenor even of situations with seemingly inevitably sad endings. Such was the case with Mal, who bravely fought terminal cancer. Terminally ill clients often feel that they are not in charge of their own lives. Their illness, their physicians, and their caregivers often exert much influence over what the clients can and cannot do. Because SFBT is organized around helping clients identify, express, and implement what they want, it is a comforting contrast to the experience most terminally ill people have of being repeatedly "told what to do." In this case, the therapist respectfully supported Mal in arranging her life in her own best way. The results were dramatic, although the change happened in small, incremental steps.

Although I can no longer exactly recall her features, when I think of Mal I picture those comfortable sweatshirts with pictures of teddy bears, birds, or flowers. An intelligent, avid reader with lively curiosity, she always had a book with her and much to share from her reading. And the hats—some outrageous, some whimsical, and some even downright cute and so touchable! She'd been bald at least three times and had accumulated a wardrobe of hats to cover chemotherapy's unwelcome trademark. She was always cheerful with the office staff, regardless of how she felt physically or emotionally. Over the two years we worked together we developed a special bond. I loved her and she loved me. If she were alive today, with her customary self-deprecation, she'd find it difficult to accept that I found working with her to be an inspirational, educational, and humbling privilege. I think what she taught me was that courage doesn't necessarily come in big bold moves or bravado. She showed me how small changes, in the context of a loving relationship, can have tremendous power. And when she took control toward the end of her life, I was awestruck. So how can her story be considered a triumph when, in the end, she died? This story is a tribute to her.

Mary Alice was 58 when I first met her in February of 1994. "Call me Mal," she said. It was a lucky match. We were only a few months apart in age, we had husbands in the same profession, we were both mothers of adult children. We had an immediate connection. She'd been referred to me by the social worker in the oncology clinic at a large hospital where I'd given a workshop on collaborative therapy. Because of her insurance, I saw her at an outpatient clinic rather than in my private practice office.

Her ovarian cancer, diagnosed in 1988, had recurred in the autumn of 1993 and had spread. Following surgery, chemotherapy, and radiation treatments, she enjoyed four years of remission. Now, after a third surgery and round of treatments, her doctor had suggested she concentrate on "the quality of life." She had just completed the latest chemotherapy treatment, with its theft of her energy and hair, and her doctor thought she needed someone outside her family to talk with. Feeling frightened, discouraged, depressed, and anxious, she characteristically didn't want to burden her husband or kids and followed her doctor's advice.

Mal had been driving herself to the hospital some thirty minutes away for the daily regimen of chemotherapy, refusing the social worker's suggestion to ask her family to take time from work to help. I wasn't sure how she had the strength to do this, but she was adamant about protecting her family from obligations for her care. Within her circle of long-standing and caring friends, she was "embarrassed" to talk about cancer again because she felt like "the boy who cried wolf." She was afraid she had exhausted the energy and compassion of her many friends.

Mal told me that the social worker at the oncology clinic had described her as "codependent." A catch phrase from the field of substance abuse therapy, the term had negative connotations. But Mal had decided that the term fit her. Tearful and agitated, she explained that she'd lived her life "caretaking" others, working hard to please and to win approval from those around her. She added that, since others' needs and demands kept changing, she was "exhausted" with the effort of "bouncing off others" and "performing" to keep their approval or avoid their disapproval all her life. She described herself as having two parts—one part that "grovels" and another part that has "fun and wants to help others but goes too far."

When I asked her how she wanted counseling to be helpful to her, she said she wanted to learn to live life on her own terms, to become more relaxed and honest with "who I am and how I am." She said she wanted to make the most of the time she had left and to "die a good death." When I asked what that would mean for her, she said that the people she loved would know how truly loved they were, and that she would have sorted out her spiritual *questions and made her peace with God. Her biggest worry was her family and whether they could deal with her illness and eventual death.*

We met about twice a month from the spring of 1994 through the summer of 1996. At times cancer gave her a reprieve and she felt energetic and well. Other times, her blood counts controlled the need for further chemotherapy treatments, and she felt too ill or tired to see me. She knew every detail of her treatment—all the medications and what all the numbers meant. Sometimes she said she was fed up with her doctor's appointments and simply wanted to stay home.

Although she found it disgusting and uncomfortable to talk about herself so much, she said she needed a place where she could be totally honest. At first she was worried about everything she said, wondering what I would think about her. Eventually she felt she could be honest in our meetings, which she appreciated. As was my practice, each time we met I asked how she wanted the meeting to be helpful to her that day, and I followed her lead, asking questions and accepting whatever she told me about herself. I saw my role as that of a tool or facilitator for her to use in whatever way she found most helpful. I maintained a stance of collaboration and respect for her as the expert in her own life. At times, this meant I had to fight my own agenda in favor of hers.

She found pleasure in the small and ordinary beauties of life. With her zest and humor, we often found things to laugh about together. She was unconditional in her love for her children, but struggled with love/hate in other significant relationships, sometimes guiltily expressing anger or resentment about them. In many of our meetings she struggled with feelings of inadequacy and uncertainty about herself. Sometimes I shared stories from my own life or others I knew or had worked with, which I hoped would illustrate the universal human nature of such struggles.

One story I shared with her was about a social worker I knew who had died of cancer after a nine-year battle. I told her how Bernice had decided she would have her last summer at the lake and wouldn't die until she finished a project of great importance to her: bringing Gilda's Club to her area. Gilda's Club was a community program inspired by the late comedienne Gilda Radner, who had ovarian cancer. Before she died, Gilda had wanted to have a comfortable, supportive place where people diagnosed and living with cancer could spend time with each other and their families in pleasant, nonmedical surroundings. Gilda's Club in California became an inspiration for similar homes in other states, and my friend Bernice was on a committee to establish such a club in her community. She had decided she wouldn't die until her work was well on its way. And that was how it happened. Mal found this true story unbelievable and couldn't imagine how anyone could take control in that way.

Because so much of my work seemed to move along briskly and end in a relatively short time, Mal's process felt very slow. However, I had also worked on a long-term basis with a number of people, and I accepted that Mal's struggle with cancer played a role in her evolving story. I always listened for and asked about her strengths and the smallest of changes—what she thought about them, how she was able to do them, what she thought they meant about her, and where she thought they came from.

The conversations that emerged seemed to affect the story she told of herself and enrich her self-image. By the end of each meeting, she had figured out some way to feel better about things. But the next time we met, it seemed the old story had again taken over. Whenever she expressed anger or resentment about someone in her life, guilt and remorse would immediately follow. This interested me and I asked her about it. Mal thought her early life experience had made her vulnerable to the guilt and remorse.

The oldest of several daughters born to a devout family with money and prestige, Mal had always compared herself to her "petite and proper" mother and felt like an "ugly duckling." As a teen, she entered a seven-year training in a convent to become a nun, knowing this pleased her parents. However, in her sixth year of training she decided it was the wrong choice for her and, knowing her parents would be disappointed, made the tough decision to leave. Her father told her she had "shamed" her family and she felt sinfully selfish.

Despite the fact that she went on to earn a university degree and teach for a number of years, Mal carried the feeling of shame and inadequacy with her. She concluded that these feelings were what *pushed her to always look for approval, and she wanted to change in order to find "peace" in her life. From what the doctors had been telling her, she needed to hurry. But she found it difficult to change. She continued caretaking her elderly, now widowed, mother and stopped her own chemotherapy treatments when her husband required medical treatment and surgery.*

Inwardly, Mal struggled with her negative self-judgment, which seemed to plague and stifle her. She would ruminate over things she'd said or done, wondering if she'd offended someone. To everyone else, however, she seemed free and open, loving and giving. When undergoing chemotherapy treatments at the clinic, she usually baked cookies or brought some other homemade treat for the nurses and doctors, whom she adored. She joked with the good-looking young doctor in a charming way, while turning her care over to the older, more experienced doctor.

She was chatty and interested in the other patients she saw regularly. A support group and "community" for each other, she called them and herself "frequent fliers." At holiday time she made a large wreath for the clinic wall. While undergoing chemotherapy treatments, which lasted several hours, she sometimes wrote short notes to friends or to me on bright cards decorated with cartoon figures or photos of little children. During one phase, she undertook her own fund-raising campaign for the cancer clinic by sending letters to everyone she knew, praising the clinic and the staff and requesting donations. She raised a significant amount of money.

After we'd been meeting for a while, Mal decided she could try to be a little more open and honest with family and friends. "After all," she said, "what have I got to lose?" She began making small changes. She called it "being assertive." She reported that her husband called it "making trouble." We laughed about it together. She spoke often about religion, which she thought was very personal, and described herself as a "seeker." She visited several churches and clergymen, searching for a spiritual home that felt right to her. In our meetings, she didn't often speak directly about cancer or about death.

She said that although cancer hung over her head, it also had given her gifts. I wondered if some of the strengths I saw were among these. For instance, the social worker at the hospital thought Mal should invite her family to a meeting so they could talk about what was happening, but she refused, not wanting to burden them with what she knew would be very painful for them. Although I agreed with the hospital worker, I respected Mal's choice and was amazed at her strength when it came to protecting her family. She consistently held true to this, even as she struggled with her ambivalence about other things.

In our second year of work together, Mal's symptoms began to bother her more. Experiencing some discomfort and pain, she sometimes canceled appointments, and the time between appointments stretched longer. When she didn't come in, she kept in touch with short phone calls or brief notes. And when I hadn't heard from her for a while, I would call her. She told me how she'd begun respecting her body's need for rest, and sometimes stopped working—something she never would have done before. She also began saying a little more about what she needed or wanted from her husband and best friend. She said "no" when she didn't want to do something—a fairly new experience for her—and found it both disturbing and liberating. She invited her husband to a meeting and was nervous as a cat, hoping he'd like me. Afterwards she had second thoughts because she'd expressed anger at him in our meetings and now I could see "what a wonderful and loving man he is—a pussycat." Each time we met or spoke, I heard more and more changes. It was exciting to witness.

One day Mal called with stunning news. She had decided to stop the treatments. She told me she knew the cancer was outrunning the treatments, and her discomfort was increasing. She was now taking pain medication regularly and felt she would no longer be able to come to see me. She said she was ready for the end. She had called hospice and had signed on as a client. She had made the decision alone and had not discussed it with anyone. She had invited a hospice nurse to her home to speak with her family, and had informed her husband and children about the meeting. She had taken charge calmly and with authority.

Her taking charge took my breath away. One the one hand, I was grief stricken, but on the other, I was jubilant. We cried together on the telephone. I gave her my support and told her she *could call at any time. When the hospice worker met with the family, her husband later told me, he didn't know what signing on with hospice meant. He learned that Mal had decided to cease further treatment and to receive only palliative care in her home until the inevitable end. It was a shock for him and their children, but they accepted her choice.*

Mal was under hospice care for about two months. I visited her at her home. She was weak and a bit angry at herself for having no energy. After we spoke about it and I reminded her that cancer was an energy robber, she decided to "not beat [herself] up about it." The only thing she felt bad about was the pain she knew her family was feeling, which she knew was now unavoidable.

As we talked, it seemed she had met all the goals she had set out when we first started together. She had learned to live life on her own terms—calling hospice was the ultimate proof of that. She had undertaken a spiritual quest and had made peace with God. She felt she had made the most of the time she had left, and her family and friends knew, without a doubt, how much she loved them. She had stocked her cupboards with food and cleaning supplies, and had filled a small wicker basket on her desk with birthday and other cards filed under the appropriate dates for her husband to mail throughout the year. She had decided where and how she wanted her funeral, and had spoken with the clergyman whom she wanted to officiate. She was prepared for "a good death." She hugged me and asked her husband to show me his garden as we said good-bye. It was a beautiful garden, filled with prize-winning flowers, and I remember the poignant feeling as her husband and I walked in the warm sunshine before I left.

I didn't visit again. I spoke briefly to her husband when I called; Mal was usually asleep or not up to talking. She was extremely tired and went in and out of lucidity. Her family and friends drew near. On the day she died, she and her husband held hands and said a prayer. At her funeral, which I attended in my lonely grief, the church was overflowing. There were tunes she had selected, and people who knew her shared poems about her. There were family members, friends, neighbors, doctors, and nurses from the cancer clinic, as well as other patients and their families—people of all ages. Her children spoke and it was obvious that her love was something they would never lose. I hoped that she somehow knew how beloved she was—that she could see how many people she had so profoundly touched, me among them.

Mal's courage and profoundly loving heart are truly inspiring, as is the therapist's graceful skill in consistently providing a respectful context from which Mal could direct the course of her therapy and decide what the most meaningful ways to spend the precious remaining time of her life were. As the next story shows, not all clients have goals as admirable as those of Mal, but small changes can sometimes produce results that ultimately are more commendable than one might anticipate.

Not Having to Love Her
Contributed by Therese Steiner, M.D., Zurich, Switzerland

Mr. and Mrs. Meyer, parents of three adopted children from Colombia, came to see me. Two of the children were twin boys and the third child was the boys' half-sister Cecilia. I had treated Cecilia in play therapy with good results about a year and half earlier, and I wondered what could be wrong with the children. It turned out that Mrs. Meyer had experienced a great deal of difficulty with Cecilia, and this was the first time she honestly told me that "even though I brought her to therapy to you before, maybe it wasn't her but me who needed help."

Mrs. Meyer was very troubled by 5-year-old Cecilia's poor table manners and the hassle she created around eating. No matter how much Mrs. Meyer tried to teach Cecilia table manners, the little girl completely ignored her. Mrs. Meyer complained bitterly that Cecilia never ate when told to eat and that she refused to talk to her mother. She explained that originally another family had planned to adopt Cecilia. However, both the adoption agency and her own family had exerted a lot of pressure to keep the three siblings together, and she had reluctantly agreed to adopt Cecilia in addition to the twins.

It was becoming clear to me that the mother did not really like Cecilia. Though she knew that Cecilia suffered a serious, sustained period of hunger as a young child, Mrs. Meyer showed no compassion or emotional attachment toward her daughter. Mrs. Meyer was torn between feeling repulsed by the child and feeling guilty and disturbed by her negative reaction to this little girl who needed so much help from her. She never had any complaints about her twin sons. I asked Mrs. Meyer when she felt good about Cecilia. It was rather disturbing to hear that she felt good about her daughter only when Cecilia was away or being taken care of by someone else (such as her grandparents or her aunt); when Cecilia smiled at her or someone else in the family; when she "didn't have to like her, she just had to tolerate her"; when she didn't "make an effort to talk to her, be nice to her, or convince her to eat or play"; and when "the distance between us is there and I don't feel the pressure to narrow it."

At the end of the meeting, I reassured Mrs. Meyer that her goal of just wanting to learn to tolerate Cecilia, and not having to like or love her, made sense and was a reasonable goal. She seemed relieved.

Mrs. Meyer came to the next session alone and she was much more frank about her goal of not wanting to treat the girl as a daughter but as a houseguest, and of thinking of herself as a nurse taking care of the child. We talked in great detail about what this would be like. What behaviors would she be doing in order to accomplish the various tasks of acting like Cecilia's nurse and not having to love her? At the end of the session, Mrs. Meyer said that she planned to inform her husband about her decision to tolerate, not love, Cecilia.

Mr. Meyer came in alone for the next session. He explained that he came from a "patchwork family," in which he had lived with his mother and his stepfather, and he really wanted this adoption to work. He had no difficulty loving Cecilia and was disappointed by his wife's dislike of such a helpless little girl who suffered so much at a young age. I normalized his wife's reaction to Cecilia and reassured him that there are many different ways to adequately parent a child and somehow they all seem to work out.

Mr. Meyer told me that he would have to make up for his wife's missing affection for Cecilia—that he would have to be the mother. I agreed it was a wonderful idea and said there was no reason why fathers could not be good mothers. We discussed some of his concrete, detailed ideas about how to be a mother to Cecilia. Within the next few days, Mrs. Meyer telephoned to say that she was truly grateful to me for helping her and her husband and that she was confident that things would work out for her family.

Although it may have been difficult, by not interfering with Mrs. Meyer's goals the therapist normalized the mother's dislike of the adopted daughter, thus staying away from claiming a moral high ground. It's possible that the situation already was being worsened by the mother's anxiety about feeling repulsed by the daughter she felt she was supposed to love. Normalizing the mother's feelings helped free Mrs. Meyer of her guilt, thereby enabling her to find a way to relate as a caregiver to her daughter. By avoiding a stance that would force Mrs. Meyer to "confront her feelings" about Cecilia, the therapist raised the possibility of the mother's eventually getting to the same spot (loving her daughter) by another path. Additionally, by acknowledging rather than judging or criticizing the mother's feelings, the therapist may well have saved Cecilia the further trauma of a failed adoption or even physical neglect by her adoptive mother. I hope that the fact that Mrs. Meyer is no longer "trying" to love this little girl will somehow free her to begin developing more positive feelings toward Cecilia. As the Chinese saying goes, "A journey of a thousand miles begins with a first step."

Chapter 9

KID'S STUFF: STORIES ABOUT SFBT WITH CHILDREN

Working with children in a solution-focused manner is both similar to and different from therapy with adults. The similarities lie in the posture we hold toward the client: taking a collaborative stance; assuming competence and good intentions; seeing the client, even a child, as the expert; taking a not-knowing posture; and allowing the client to generate his/her own solutions as much as possible. Much of this is conveyed nonverbally. The major difference lies in deciding which tools to use and how to make them fit the children's needs, much as, when teaching children to play violin, one uses a smaller violin to fit their small hands, short arms, and so on.

Sophisticated and/or abstract concepts may need to be translated into words or concepts that are familiar to children and fit their level of language and cognitive development. For example, when introducing the miracle question, we might talk of magic wands or fairy godmothers, or even wave a toy magic wand filled with colorful sparkling stars. Scaling questions are easily adapted. For instance, 1 to 10 can be shown with drawings of different facial expressions, from a broad smile to a frown, or a stepladder reaching for the sky, or a yellow brick road leading to the land of Oz.

In working with children in a group, a therapist can have the children stand up, choose one side of the wall to stand for 1 and the opposite wall for 10, and then literally move around to indicate their level of problems, successes, courage, bravery, and so on. Some very sensitive child protective services workers have devised a slide that shows numbers 1 to 10 and a pull-out tab that can slide back and forth to indicate the level of safety, fear of abusive person, or attachment to the parenting figures in a child's life. The creative adaptation of scaling questions is limitless.

The Truck Driver who Needed Help
Contributed by Robin McCarthy, Portland, Maine

Whether we use talk or play therapy, with adults or children, the ultimate goal of therapy is to enhance the client's sense of competence, mastery over life's difficulties, and a sense of safety, comfort, and control over one's life. SFBT's assumption that clients are the experts on their own lives holds true even when working with children who have limited verbal skill to handle some of the cognitive concepts. In this chapter we describe how talented therapists adapt play therapy, sand trays, puppets, and other useful tools when working with children, even those who have been traumatized, such as Timothy in the following story. McCarthy shows how a therapist's acceptance, creativity, and imaginative enactment empower a child's discovery of a solution that is simple, painless, and fitting.

Rachel brought her four-and-a-half-year-old son Timothy to see me because he was enuretic and encopretic. Rachel had left Arthur, Timothy's father, after he had beaten her in front of the children. Subsequently, Rachel found that when the kids were visiting Arthur, he spanked them and used other forms of corporal punishment that were unacceptable to her. Rachel decided to seek full custody of the children, with Arthur having supervised visits only. Arthur committed suicide. Following this event, Timothy lost control of his bowels and bladder.

Timmy didn't want to talk about any of it. At our third session, Timothy and I played in the sandbox with toy trucks. I was frantically thinking about how trucks could have a relationship to playing out encopresis or enuresis. Then I had an idea. I said in a "tough guy" truck driver voice, "Hey, buddy, let's take a coffee break." Timothy responded in a gruff tone, "Okay." Still using my truck driver voice, I asked where the bathroom was because "I needed to poop." I made loud (pretend) bathroom noises and pooping and farting noises. Then we got back into our trucks and back to work.

We continued playing with the trucks and using the voices for quite a while, until I felt we had bonded as fellow truck drivers. Then I said in my truck driver voice, "Hey buddy, I have a problem that's really embarrassing to talk about. Can I talk to you?" "Sure," Timothy responded. I continued with how embarrassed I was and how personal it was. Timothy continued to be open to hearing about it. Then I hesitantly said, "Well, the thing is, I keep peeing and pooping in my pants, and well, gosh, it's so embarrassing and I'm so ashamed telling you, but I just don't know what to do and I wondered if you could help me. Do you have any ideas about how I can stop peeing and pooping in my pants? What would you do? You gotta help me buddy. Please, tell me how you know when you start to have the feeling that you need to pee or poop?"

Timothy answered in his truck driver voice: "It's okay buddy, here's what you do. You just start to feel a funny feeling in your tummy and then you go right to the bathroom to see if it's pee or poop, and then you don't go in your pants anymore. That's what you do, now let's get back to work."

At Timothy's next session, Rachel told me he'd been using the toilet consistently. He solved his own problem by "helping his buddy."

The Whiz Kid
Contributed by Janet Roth, Canberra, Australia

As this case illustrates, the therapist can assume a not-knowing posture even when working with young children. Both the physically abused, emotionally weary mother and the badly abused seven-year-old child in this story could easily be seen as having no resources and no ideas about how to begin the recovery process. But the therapist's respectful posture allowed ample room for the mother and daughter to generate and act out their own solutions for making life better.

Seven-year-old Jaclyn came in full of confidence, ready to make some changes. Jaclyn's mother, Pamela, wanted the best for her daughter, but she confided that she was "no angel to live with," adding that when the pressures of life got to her she tended to lose her temper and yell and scream at Jaclyn. She was eager to learn and to keep trying new things. Pamela had escaped an abusive relationship with Jaclyn's father, and she was eager for a better, happier life. Jaclyn's father had also beaten Jaclyn, using coat hangers, electric cords, wooden spoons, and other items, but this didn't seem to dampen her spirit. She was teeming with the joy of life and had the resilience of a very wise young girl. She talked, danced, and drew pictures. When we sang songs together, she usually chose "Twinkle, Twinkle, Little Star." This choice pleased me because it was one of the few songs I sing well.

Jaclyn loved jazz dancing and performing, playing on the monkey bars at school, and playing chase with her friends on the schoolyard. There was just one thing that kept getting her into trouble: She desperately wanted to "get Daddy out of my mind."

We discovered that she had "two" daddies: "naughty Daddy" and "good Daddy." Naughty Daddy often came at bedtime and gave Jaclyn nightmares. Sometimes he made her do very bad things at school, like have severe tantrums and throw furniture. He made it hard for her to get along with friends, and she often felt jealous when others did well or received awards. Naughty Daddy also gave her bad moods at home, and she would get into trouble with her mother. Good Daddy played ballgames with her and sometimes took her to the park and other places. At the time of our first meeting, Jaclyn had not seen her father in about six months, following a traumatic, abusive incident while visiting him.

Jaclyn had many ideas about how to resolve her problems with naughty Daddy, and her mother was surprised at how strongly she featured in them. The best ideas came from Jaclyn herself: lots of cuddles and kisses with Mum, talking and doing things with Mum, helping Mum at home to earn some pocket money, having a hot water bottle to help stay in bed, having friends over and going to friend's houses, and so on. I had one idea to offer, which incorporated Jaclyn's love of movement and music. Being a concrete thinker myself and knowing that most seven-year-olds are concrete thinkers, I wanted to explore actually getting naughty Daddy out of the way. So I suggested we play musical chairs.

It was my turn to be surprised when Jaclyn didn't know this game. I gave all three of us a Teddy bear. My Teddy was naughty Daddy. We sang "Twinkle, Twinkle, Little Star" and marched around the chairs. Of course, there were three Teddies and only two chairs, and naughty Daddy missed out on a chair at the end of the song, in spite of trying very hard to sit down in one! Jaclyn wanted to do it again and again.

Because Jaclyn liked ballgames and drawings, the most sensible homework to assign at the conclusion of our session seemed to be to draw a picture of naughty Daddy, crumple it up into a ball, and throw it in the wastebasket. Both Jaclyn and her mother were enthusiastic about this idea.

When they returned a month later, Pamela told me she had enrolled in a psychology course by correspondence. She said that she had learned a great deal in our first session and wanted to learn more. She thanked me. I found her response intriguing, because I didn't think I had done that much—I had just listened, played with Jaclyn, asked some questions, and searched for ideas that could become solutions. Perhaps this was what it is like to "lead from behind."

Apparently, this was enough to start the ball rolling. Pamela and Jaclyn had incorporated all of Jaclyn's ideas into their lives, and they were thrilled with the changes. Pamela now appreciated how important cuddles and kisses were to her and Jaclyn's relationship. Previously, she hadn't realized how much she had to offer Jaclyn by being available to talk and do things with her. They were enjoying each other, playing together, and had opened new patterns of communication. Pamela now listened to Jaclyn more, and Jaclyn listened to her mother more as well. During our first session,

Pamela had noticed what excellent ideas Jaclyn had, and she now said she would "think before telling her off."

Pamela pointed out that Jaclyn was a "whiz kid," and we all agreed. Jaclyn was beaming and excited. We also commented on her bravery, as she was going to be visiting her father in a few days. Together we made a safety plan, again using all of Jaclyn's ideas. She even thought of clues, like Daddy's tone of voice, that could alert her to seek safety. She insisted that we play musical chairs again. So we did.

Jaclyn's visit with her father never took place because he became abusive over the telephone to Pamela. He was insisting on taking Jaclyn overnight, but Pamela, protective of Jaclyn, would not allow it. This caused a setback for Jaclyn, who could hear the argument from her bedroom. Naughty Daddy was back in her head, "saying nasty things" and causing problems at school. Jaclyn described it in a couple of letters she wrote to me while she was in school. These letters appear on pages 150–151.

Jaclyn did not want to see her father but struggled with missing the things she enjoyed doing with him, like playing with her half-brothers. She thought that someday she might want to telephone and ask to play, but not yet. She seemed relieved that this could be an option and that it could be within her control.

Things had remained on a positive note at home, so we capitalized on this and decided to "bring Mum to school" by sending love notes in Jaclyn's lunchbox. Once again, they were both excited about this idea, and Jaclyn was sure that the notes would "surprise me and make me think of Mum and be happy. I'd have a better day, knuckle down, and do my work." We used the Teddy bear scale (10 teddies cut out of fabric) to talk about how much love there was in Jaclyn's life.

At this point, Jaclyn independently decided to consult my colleague, Winnie-the-Pooh (McCleod, 1986). Once again, Jaclyn was demonstrating her ability to know exactly what would be most helpful to her. But Winnie has a very, very quiet voice, that comes from the pillow in my room covered in Winnie-the-Pooh fabric. Jaclyn put her ear to the pillow and listened very hard to what Winnie had to say. She informed me, "Winnie-the-Pooh wants me

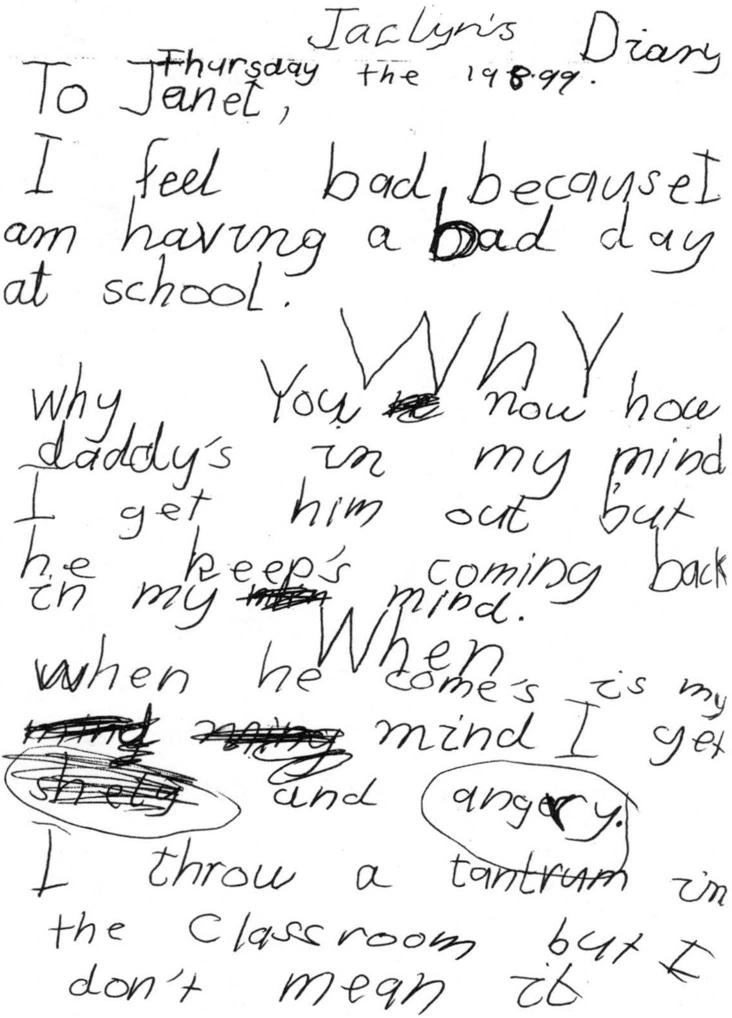

Jaclyn's Diary

Thursday the 19.8.99.

To Janet,

I feel bad, because I am having a bad day at school.

WHY

why You now how daddy's in my mind I get him out but he keep's coming back in my ~~min~~ mind.

When

when he come's is my ~~mind~~ ~~ming~~ mind I get ~~shely~~ and angry.

I throw a tantrum in the Classroom but I don't mean it

Figure 1: Jaclyn's first letter

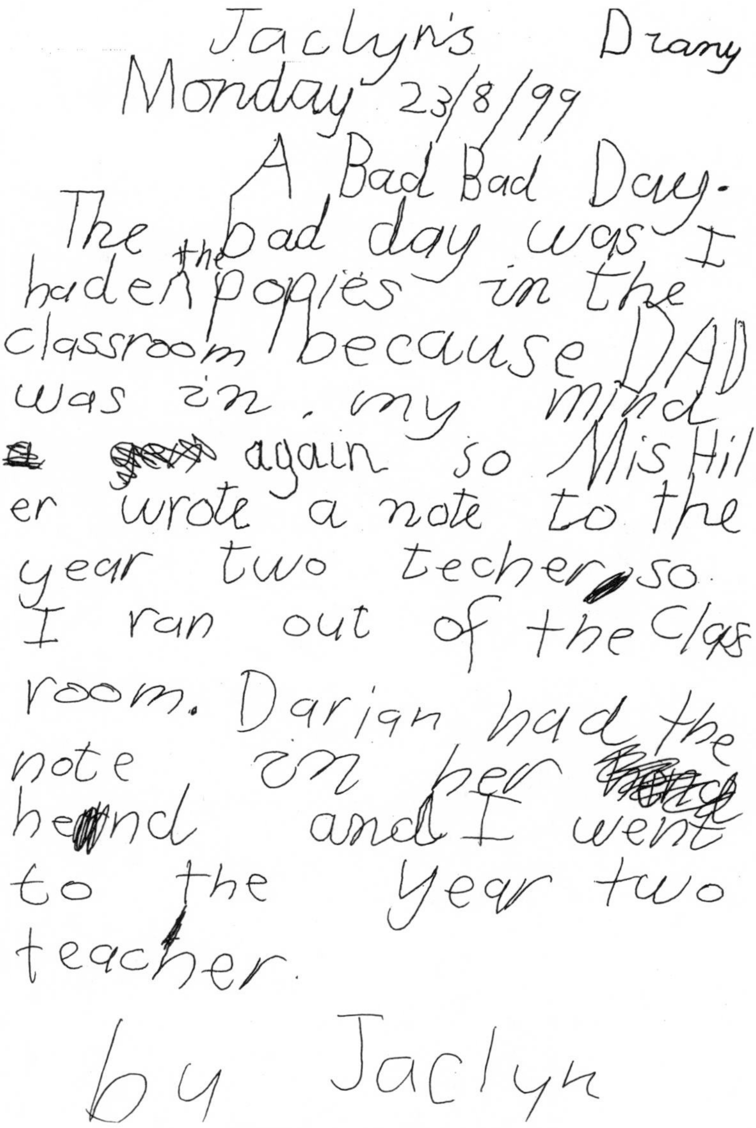

Jaclyn's Drany
Monday 23/8/99
A Bad Bad Day.
The the bad day was I
had en popies in the
classroom because DAD
was in my mind
again so Mis Hil
er wrote a note to the
year two techer so
I ran out of the Clas
room. Darian had the
note in her
heand and I went
to the year two
teacher.
by Jaclyn

Figure 2: Jaclyn's second letter

to behave at school, at home, and at my friend's." We talked about how she would best do her "job as a kid," which was "to have fun" (McCleod, 1986).

A month later, Jaclyn and Pamela came in to say that they were both doing much better at having fun, that the tantrums at school had stopped, and that naughty Daddy was no longer getting into Jaclyn's head. The love notes in the lunchbox had become something very special between them, and sometimes even chocolates appeared! The nightmares were gone, and instead Jaclyn had dreams about Teddy bears, fairies, Barbies, and me. Jaclyn and I made playdough badges to celebrate the fun and happiness that was now in her life. We agreed to catch up in a few months.

During the interval, Pamela came in once on her own because stress was "taking over her life," much as it had two years earlier, when she had had a "breakdown." She wanted to resolve issues as they arose, rather than letting them build up until she exploded. A neighbor had recently called the police during one of Pamela's explosions at Jaclyn. She was quite distressed by this and saw it as a strong message that it was time to do something different.

I asked what she had found worked to manage her stress in the past, even a little bit, and as a result of this conversation she came up with the plan. The first step was to slow herself down and map out the first and/or second actions she needed to take when faced with an unexpected problem. When asked to elaborate further on this, Pamela explained that when she felt like things were piling up on her, such as when her ex-husband called up and demanded a visit with Jaclyn, she used to "fall apart," thinking that somehow she was obligated to follow his demands immediately. She became flustered and agitated and started to scream at Jaclyn.

Since the divorce, she had learned to take a deep breath, walk around the house a few times, and slow herself down before deciding how to respond to his demands. Other times she found it helpful to make a phone call to her best friend, her mother, or another supportive person, talk the situation over, and hear a different perspective. She knew that it helped to get accurate information before jumping to a conclusion and to recognize when she was under pressure from different sources, such as from her part-time job or friends calling needing her help, or when Jaclyn became cranky and needed extra attention. She had difficulty recognizing when she felt stretched to a limit. We discussed some signs of building tension: headaches, tightness in her chest and shoulders, and at times even weakness in her legs and arms.

One part of the plan was to make a telephone call to a child protection social worker to get accurate information about her rights and responsibilities, so that she could remain calm when Jaclyn's father called her. Pamela thought that this would help her control the conversation. She also decided that she could always hang up on him, rather than feel obligated to stay on the phone and listen to his harangue about visitations.

Interestingly, part of Pamela's action plan involved "waiting" for his next step, rather than feeling like she had to make sure that her ex-husband's demands on her were taken care of even before he spoke, as she did for years before the divorce. Within the session, just making the plan reduced her stress considerably. Like her daughter, Pamela knew just what to do to create her own solutions. She telephoned a couple of weeks later with good news: She had taken all the necessary steps to resolve the issue that had been burdening her. She also informed me, with delight, that she was doing something special for herself every day! I never had the opportunity to discuss Pamela's explosion with Jaclyn, but the next time we saw each other things were going well.

At our fifth and last session (although they know they can return anytime), Pamela felt that both her and Jaclyn's lives had improved 100 percent. Jaclyn reported that it was now easy to keep naughty Daddy out of her head. She was completing her work at school and getting good grades. She also was playing well with other children and able to celebrate her own and other children's accomplishments. Pamela was following her own advice by being more relaxed, doing something special for herself every day, and taking vitamins instead of medication. Pamela and Jaclyn's relationship was now characterized by mutual respect because they were listening to each other. The last I heard, they were heading to New Zealand for holiday.

Figure 3: Jaclyn's picture during the last (fifth) session

Getting Rid of the Monsters
Contributed by Jüergen Hargens, Meyn, Germany

Although some children, like Jaclyn, come to their first session with ideas for solutions already in mind, other children may feel overwhelmed and need encouragement before they can even begin the solution development process. This was the case with Sophie, the girl in this story. Sophie's sensitive therapist co-created a solution with her in such a way that Sophie felt comfortable crediting herself with its discovery. As is true with adult clients, children who understand that they have generated or helped generate their own solutions to their problems are the most likely to be helped by those solutions.

One Sunday night I got a call from 13-year-old Sophie. She had seen me once some time earlier and now wanted some help with a different problem. Sophie was uneasy about describing her problem. She wondered whether it was a real problem or just her imagination. So I asked her about the details of what had brought her to me: her fear of monsters. I took her problem seriously and acknowledged

her descriptions, her fears, her anxiety, and all of her previous ef-
forts to overcome the problem. Listening to her description led to
many ideas of what solutions might be possible. Afterward, I invited
Sophie to write down her experience. The following is her own
writing:

About two or three months ago I started to become fearful every
evening, and sometimes even during the day when I was alone.
Each evening when I entered my bedroom, I had the feeling that
there were monsters there. I imagined that they looked like figures
from the movie Scream 2. Horrible pictures formed in my mind
and I couldn't get rid of them. I was afraid these "monsters" would
harm me, hurt me, kill me, or the worst, would just look angrily
at me. I even started to hate my Teddy bear because I thought a
monster called "It" [from a Stephen King novel] was inside the
bear, looking incredibly angry at me.

I already knew that I couldn't stand horror movies, and I had
not watched one for a long time. But sometimes even just hearing
a story about a monster would cause me to create very frighten-
ing images in my mind. As soon as I lay in my bed at night and
turned off the light, I became so terrified of these monsters (which
I imagined were standing over me, about to kill me) that I either
hid under the blankets or immediately turned the light on again. I
scarcely dared to breathe for fear these creatures would hear, and
then even more of them could come. Strangely, however, these
thoughts only happened when I was alone. If another person was
with me, I wasn't afraid.

Common sense told me that I imagined monsters that did not
exist, but deep inside I wasn't convinced. Sometimes I thought my
problem would go away by itself, that I just needed a little more
time. But it didn't. Eventually I admitted to myself that it was not
just a small problem. I told both my sister and my best girlfriend
about it. They thought about it for quite some time, and both suggested that I should see a psychologist. So I talked to my parents
and they also thought that it would be the best for me to see Jürgen,
because they couldn't help me either. I decided to see him because
first, I couldn't find any other solution, and second, he had been
able to help me with a problem in the past.

At the beginning of our session, Jüergen explained, "I will ask many questions but if you don't want to answer any of them, please feel free to say so." That felt good! Telling him about my fear of monsters was hard. I was embarrassed to be having this fear at 13 years old. I had made up my mind ahead of time not to cry during the session, but I did anyway. But it felt good, very good. Jüergen asked many questions. Among other things, he asked how I knew that these monsters were not afraid of me and whether I had considered that maybe they were trying to frighten me in order to hide their own fear. That made me think. We talked for a long time about how to drive these monsters away or how to intimidate them. I said that I felt stupid for being afraid of monsters, but Jüergen said that I did not need to feel stupid because these monsters did exist for me. Somehow that gave me courage.

After about an hour I decided that from now on, anytime I felt that the monsters might be around, I would just speak up and tell them how cowardly they were for remaining invisible and not talking loudly. I was very satisfied with this decision, but I felt stupid that Jüergen had solved the problem for me and that I didn't find the solution for myself. But he replied that that wasn't true; I had solved the problem myself. Finding the solution had only been possible because I had thought about it for such a long time. Somehow I agreed. Leaving the room I felt terrific and totally relieved.

At home I tried my new "weapon" against the rascals the same night. Even now (about one month later) I sometimes enter my room, shocking them by yelling everything that comes into my mind: "Well you idiots! Do you know that you are the meanest and most cowardly pigs I ever met?! If you want something, show yourselves! Or don't you have enough courage?!! Ha, piss off!" Having yelled this, I didn't have any more fear.

With her therapist's support, Sophie was able to develop a solution to her imaginary monsters in just one session! How lucky she was to have found a therapist who did not become locked into the idea that she was suffering from delusions and therefore needed extensive testing or medication.

Solution Gestures:
"Circle People Who Haven't Been Bullying You"
Contributed by Keizo Hasegawa, Nagoya, Japan

This story about a girl and her teacher demonstrates a simple, clever, nonverbal way of utilizing exceptions to problems. The intervention embodies many of the signature characteristics of SFBT: it's respectful, appears elegantly simple, and of course, it *worked*!

A middle school girl complained to the class teacher that she was being bullied and shunned by her classmates. She said that she didn't want to come to school anymore. Most teachers in this situation would be eager to investigate whether the bullying is actually occurring and, if it is, to identify the bully. This teacher did neither.

The teacher listened respectfully to the girl's problem and then gave her a list of the names of the students in her class. She asked the girl to circle with a red pencil the names of those who were not bullying her. When the number of big red circles approached five, the girl voluntarily decided to go back to class. In this intervention, the visual image of the red circles was emphasized rather than the problem.

In a therapeutic setting, we would probably use language to search for a solution to a problem like this: "Tell me about the times you haven't been bullied." But nonverbal methods can work in many cases and with clients of any age.

HOW DOES ONE DEAL WITH PARENTS WHO "SABOTAGE" THEIR CHILD'S TREATMENT?

Having consulted with many treatment programs that provide services to children, we have come across many professionals who raise this kind of question. They report that parents often miss the child's appointment, use flimsy excuses for failing to follow through on treatment recommendations, terminate contracts with the clinician just when the therapy seems to be getting into some "real" issues, or complain bitterly about the child even though the child is making good progress in treatment. These parents are frequently described as "sabotaging" the child's therapy.

"Sabotage" is one of those unfortunate words that we professionals use to describe clients (or parents) who are viewed as behaving counter to their best interests for some dark, obscure reason. This kind of thinking comes from an individualistic, linear way of looking at how people function and operate. We propose that everyone operates within the context of relationship and nothing stands on its own.

When one is focused on children's serious problems, it is easy to lose sight of the important roles parents play in these children's lives. When practitioners think from a causal relationship frame, it is easy to blame parents without realizing that they are doing so. After all, the common wisdom says that children's strengths and problems are shaped by their parents, and so when we are faced with glaring problems in small children, it is easy to blame the parents. Even though the parents may deny it, they, too, may wonder and worry about their part in the child's problems. Of course, if clinicians assume parental responsibility, they will unwittingly communicate that view to the parents, making things much worse than they need to be.

When working with children, therefore, it is particularly important to view the parents as cotherapists or consultants. After all, at the end of the therapeutic intervention, whether outpatient or residential, the child ultimately goes home to live with his or her parent. And who loves and knows the child better than his orher own parent? From this perspective, it is easy to cooperate with the parents first and always treat them as the experts on their child that they are. Any credit for the progress the child makes in treatment should always be given to the parents first, then to the child. When children hear that his or her parents have done something successfully, it has a tremendous impact on them. We have known numerous examples on videotape of how children immediately seem to calm down and become more attentive. Of course, complimenting the children directly also seems to act as an indirect compliment to parents since they see their children as reflections of their parenting.

Progress is seen as based on the foundation of love and caring the parents have given the child from the beginning and you have only helped to blossom now. For example, the more parents complain about the child, the more you need to compliment them on maintaining such strong hope for the child, that in spite of the difficulties they have experienced, they still believe that the child can improve someday. Of course, this expression of hope is very reassuring to the child.

We believe that words that attribute negative motivations to the clients such as "sabotage" or "resistive" or "minimize the problems," are generally not useful for treatment. They do not generate hope for the child or the parent.

Chapter 10

GOING SLOWLY ON THE RIGHT TRACK

The last story of this book is sad and touching in many ways, because it describes the struggles of a young man who is approaching middle age, with a long history of mental illness and involvement with the mental health system. In spite of all the odds against him, Steven struggles to maintain his dignity and his sense of wanting to do the right thing, and he eventually succeeds within his ability. Reading his long, tortuous journey is poignant, because in a child-like way he tries to do good and be useful to himself and others. We begin to appreciate his parents' and sister's pain, love, and commitment to him. They have stood by him in such a way that Steven has had no doubts about their love and support.

This story shows all the SFBT techniques we have described in this book used with consistent respect. The therapist and the team allowed Steven to shape his future, by carefully observing him making choices within what was given to him. We cannot help but admire his ability to learn, to change, and make the most of what he has.

Two Different Stories, Same Steven
Contributed by Joel K. Simon, Walden, New York

Steven, the youngest of six children, was born in New York City to working-class parents. The family moved to the mid-Hudson region of New York state when Steven was 13. He was 38 years old when I first met him. He had been a patient in the mental health system for 21 years, since he was 17 years old, even though he related that his "mental" problems started in early childhood (perhaps 6 or 7 years) and reported that he had been a "schizophrenic" all his life. He had had multiple hospitalizations in community and state psychiatric institutions; his average hospital stay ranged from three to eight weeks. Four psychiatric evaluations completed by four different psychiatrists diagnosed Steven as schizophrenic, chronic, undifferentiated type. He had been on a variety of psychiatric medications, many of which produced side effects.

Frustrated, the psychiatrist at the hospital referred Steven to the county psychiatric clinic, where we met for the first time in June 1996. Steve was treated by myself, with the team behind the one-way mirror and a consultation team. (Team members included Dan Gallagher, Janet Campbell, Andy Taylor, and a changing cast of interns and students during the entire time of treatment.)

When asked what he wanted from coming to therapy this time, Steven responded that he wanted to get help with his "schizophrenia." When asked how he would know that he was getting the help he needed, he said that he would be more outspoken with people. With considerable help, he expanded on this during the course of formulating answers to the miracle question: He would speak his mind, stand up to people who talked down to him, and have a job that he could keep for good. Mingled with his long history of problems, Steven was able to describe what was already helpful to him in his life: His current medication helped prevent hallucinations. When asked how he helped the medication work for him, Steven described a wide variety of activities, particularly, taking long walks, praying, and being with his friends and family. As he talked about his friends and family, he became increasingly animated. It was clear that this conversation was very different from what he had expected, and he seemed to enjoy being asked "strange" questions, informing the therapist about his hopes and dreams, his small successes, and what he knows.

Finally, he confided that his dream was never having to see the inside of a psychiatric ward again, that he was really tired of being hospitalized. When asked what made him think that this was possible, he talked about what he did, in fact, to stay out of the hospital, to stay on track, and to maintain good relationships with friends and family who supported him. At the same time, it was clear that he had some doubts, as he talked about this in a halting and hesitant manner.

In order to establish his ability to gauge his own situation, I asked Steven to rate himself on a scale where 10 represented being on track and 1 was the opposite. He responded that he was at a 10. I assumed that he meant that he was at 10 today, and indeed I was impressed with how focused, lucid, and clear-headed he was. When asked to rate himself on a scale where 10 indicated not needing therapy to continue this progress and 1 that he needed therapy, he responded that he was at a 1. The team agreed with him, not because we thought that he needed therapy but because we realized how much he was indoctrinated into the role of the patient, so that he saw himself needing therapy for the rest of his life.

After the consultation break, the team had many compliments for Steven. After pointing out the hard work he was putting in and his knowledge of what was and was not helpful for him, we made the following suggestion: "Notice what you do that keeps you on track." Steven was obviously pleased when we acknowledged his hard work and successes, but the session was a bit unsettling for him because it was not the kind of conversation he had expected. We asked him how soon he wanted to return, and he replied four weeks.

Steven returned four weeks later, reporting that he was still on track. He said that he was calmer and that his family noticed it. He continued to do the things that he had reported were helpful. Once again, he gave much credit to the medications he was taking. After listening to his description of how he stayed on track, I said, "You sure are doing lots of things to stay on track. What percent of what is working to help you stay on track is medication and what percent is your hard work?" Steven thought about it for *a while and responded that 10 percent was the medication and 90 percent was his work. Of course, I was very pleased to hear this, because it seemed like he was beginning to give himself credit for his own improvement, even though I was not clear how much he believed all this.*

Among other things, Steven expressed interest in returning to a work program that had not been successful for him in the past. I asked him what gave him the idea that he was ready, and he was able to describe his progress—no hallucinations for a while, his ability to stay on track, being healthy by taking care of himself, and keeping in touch with friends and family. When I asked him what gave him the idea that he was ready to go to work now, he replied that he was ready this time because he knew that he had come a long way from "those crazy days" and listed his accomplishments during the last four weeks. The team agreed with his view of hard work and was impressed by the program he had developed to help him stay on track. We suggested that he notice any other clues that told him that he was ready for a job program.

During the course of the next few sessions, spaced about four to six weeks apart, Steven reported that he met with the staff from the work program. In an articulate and logical manner, he explained why he felt he was ready to return to the program. Unfortunately, because of previous negative experiences with him, the program turned him down. Records indicate that one of Steven's major problems was his tendency to be obsessed with one female worker, whom he followed around, pestered, and stared at, which made her feel harassed and stalked. He was understandably disappointed at the rejection, but was willing to look into an alternative job training program.

Close to Christmas of 1996, Steven suffered the first of several defining events that occurred during our work together. His father, with whom he was very close, died from cancer. Grief stricken and yet not knowing how to console himself or get the kind of support he needed, Steven signed himself into a local community hospital mental health unit, because, as he reported later, he felt "very depressed." This was the first Christmas without his father. Steven stayed in the unit for a day and a half and then decided he no longer needed to be there. The hospital staff agreed and discharged him. Given his 21 years of history with mental health services and an average of three or four hospitalizations per year, we thought he did remarkably well.

During one meeting after his father's death, Steven talked about how much his dad meant to him and how much wisdom his father had given him. He mentioned that his father was always there for him, that he knew that his father was disappointed with Steven's "schizophrenia," and that he was very sad that his father could not help him more. He talked a great deal about what a gentle person his father was. When I asked him what would make his dad proud of him, Steven said, without hesitation, his having stayed out of the hospital so much longer and his staying only a day and a half this time. Steven related how his friends and family, especially his mom and sister, were supportive of him and how helpful it was to him. Considering his long-standing problems, I was impressed with how well he managed and how appropriate he was in coping with his loss.

In the early months of 1997, Steven pursued various options available to him, including a sheltered work program and psychosocial club called River Club, which offered rehabilitation services as well as job programs for those recovering from (chronic) mental illness. He took time to evaluate various options and was always somewhat hesitant. He reported that he had attended the River Club before. He had gone to the meetings a few times but dropped out about two years before we met. This time, however, Steven actually joined the River Club on his own initiative. He beamed as he reported having taken this step. The following is a short excerpt from a session about this topic.

> *Steven:* (Smiling) *I joined the River Club.*
> *Therapist: Oh, did you? Congratulations. All right!* (shaking his hand)
> *Steven: I thought about it for a long, long time. I kept messing around with it. Something told me to do it, and I said to my mom, "You know, I should join the River Club." She said that it would be a good idea. It would give me something to do.*
> *Therapist: Have you gone yet?*
> *Steven:* (Proudly) *I went last week. I stayed for two days.*

> *Therapist: So, what made you decide to do that?*
> *Steven: I didn't want to do that job thing. I would have to get a cab to the bus terminal in Centerville, and then get a cab from Centerville to the job. It would be too much. I don't need work right now. What I need is social.*
> *Therapist: What told you that it was a good decision?*
> *Steven: Myself. I thought about it.*
> *Therapist: So what do you like about it?*
> *Stephen: It has a job program. They have a job coach and help you find jobs in the community. They have breakfast there. They go on trips. I like that. And I get to see my friends there, which I like very much.*

During one session, Steven reported, full of pride, that he even joined the job program, an extension of the River Club, and received praise from his supervisor for his responsible behavior, such as coming to work on time, and performing his job in a responsible manner and getting along well with his supervisor and other co-workers. His job entailed sorting out used clothing donated by the community. His voice was strong and apparently he had rehearsed his words carefully so that they flowed smoothly.

In November 1997 Steven reported that he had talked to the psychiatrist about having auditory hallucinations. The psychiatrist suggested he discuss this with me, his therapist. In the course of introducing this topic, Steven said, "It happens most of the day. When I go to River Club, I don't hear it." I was amused and delighted at Steven's ability to recognize exceptions to his hallucinations and to observe himself and be able to report his findings.

> *Therapist: (With curiosity) So when you're at River Club, you don't hear it.*
> *Steven: (Wide-eyed) When I'm here, I don't hear it either.*
> *Therapist: What's different at River Club . . . what's different here?*
> *Steven: I also don't hear it at church.*
> *(This information about the church was a surprise to me because it had never come up before.)*
> *Therapist: So what's different here, and in church?*

Steven: There's noise that blocks it out. Same thing in church. When I'm alone, I hear it—it's scary. I asked my mom whether she hears it. She told me it's probably in my mind.

Therapist: What told you to ask your mom? That's impressive! You did an experiment—you did some research.

Steven: (Laughs) Yeah, I asked my mom.

Therapist: How did you figure out how to do that?

Steven: I wanted to make sure it wasn't something going on in the whole family. My sister said she didn't hear it, my mom said she didn't hear it.

Therapist: Once you found out it wasn't real, how did that change things for you?

Steven: It's still kind of scary. I know it's not real.

Therapist: That's helpful?

Steven: I don't hear it during the day, only at night.

Therapist: What other times at your house don't you hear it?

Steven: During the day, when I'm busy. My mind is on other things.

Therapist: How do you control it?

Steven: Take my medicine on time. Eat right—being a diabetic—that has something to do with it.

Therapist: How does the medicine help?

Steven: It stabilizes me, keeps me calm, and I sleep well.

Therapist: And controlling your diet. How is that helpful?

Steven: If I eat well. If I drink coffee, I hear it more. So I cut down on coffee.

Therapist: What else do you find helps?

Steven: I pray a lot. That helps. I talk to people. When I get angry, I hear it even more.

Therapist: So how do you keep from getting angry?

Steven: Go to River Club and talk to people there.

Therapist: Since you've been doing that and getting less angry, what have you noticed is different?

Steven: Look at my car models, sometimes I draw. I go to the library.

Therapist: How are these things helpful?

Steven: They help pretty good.

Therapist: What else do you find helpful?

Steven: Keeping more active and controlling it more.

Therapist: What about at night, what do you do to keep busy?

Steven: Probably keeping busier—finding things to do to keep busy.

Therapist: What could you do that would be helpful?

Steven: Exercise, do sit-ups. Read the Bible or other books.

(Shifting gears, the therapist asks the scaling question on Steven's confidence that he can follow up on all these good ideas. This technique allows the client to step out of himself and assess his own situation.)

Therapist: So, this time, on a confidence scale where 10 is you're really sure that these things will help and 1 is the opposite, where are you?

Steven: 10. The other thing is going to bed later.

Therapist: You have lots of good ideas. How did you come up with them?

Steven: That's what my dad used to tell me to do when he was living.

Therapist: What other ideas did your dad have that are helpful to you now?

Steven: He used to say many times, "Don't think too much. Don't sit around and daydream. Stay busy."

Several months later Steven initiated conversation that addressed his diagnosis and medication. The following shows the flow of his lucid mind at work.

Steven: I hope one day I can get well and get off the medication. That's what I'm looking for. I know you can't really cure schizophrenia, but you can help yourself.
I hope in two years to be off, where I won't need it anymore. At least not as much as I need now.

Therapist: So, what will tell you you're even ready to think about that?

Steven: Helping myself more.

Therapist: What will tell you that you're doing that?

Steven: Getting along with people at River Club. Do things
without depending on medication all the time.

Therapist: I'm curious. You've come such a long way. It's
been a while since you've been in the hospital for a day
and a half—that's it. You are going to the River Club,
making friends. I wonder what your mother and sister
think about all this.

Steven: My mom is very glad. My sister thinks I've come a
long way since the early eighties. Since I first got sick.
I've been getting better step by step, like building blocks.

Therapist: So, if your sister were here and I asked her,
"What is it that you think Steven is doing that has been
the most helpful to him?" What would she say?

Steven: Going to my program, being active—I don't get
cranky like I was before.

Therapist: So, would you have imagined that you would
have gotten this far?

Steven: No, I wouldn't have imagined. It's a surprise to me.

Another defining event occurred about 16 months after we began.
Apparently Steven went into a store and saw a woman clerk there
whom he found attractive. He would constantly visit the store and,
as the woman experienced it, harass her. He also began calling her
up. She finally called the police and Steven was arrested.

Therapist: You said something about Friday, some horrible
experience, and you learned something from it.

Steven: I was scared to death. All day Friday I was scared.

Therapist: I talked to Linda [staff member of River Club]
and she tells me that she suggested that you stay on the
other side of the road. Did you think that was a good
idea?

Steven: Yeah. I begged the lady to forgive me. She went to
grab the phone and I said, "I won't come in here anymore," and I walked out.

Therapist: Great idea! How did you think to do that?

("How did you think to do that?" or "How did you know
to do that?" or any question that begins with "how" implies that the client already knows what to do—think,

follow through, etc.—and we are interested in his knowledge base.)

Steven: My mind told me to do that.

Therapist: You said you learned something from this—what did you learn?

Steven: I learned you can't do things like that. You get in trouble. You can go to jail for a long time. I'm not going to do it anymore—I learned from this.

Therapist: What makes you think you can follow through on that?

Steven: I was scared to death. I expected the cops to come any minute and arrest me.

Therapist: What else?

Steven: I took Linda's advice. She told me not to go there anymore.

Therapist: Did you have a chance to test the advice out?

Steven: Yesterday. I went that way and I stayed on the other side of the street and came back on the other side.

Therapist: How did you do that?

Steven: I thought to myself that I needed to stay on the other side.

Therapist: So the advice was really helpful to you?

Steven: It was. Linda helped me a lot. I listened to her.

Therapist: My guess is this kind of thing would have landed you in the hospital in the past. (Steven nods in agreement) You ended up getting through it. How did you do it?

Steven: Taking my medicine on time. My family supported me. I told my mom.

Therapist: You told your mom? How did you have the courage to tell her?

Steven: She wasn't too worried about it and told me I shouldn't be doing it.

(The therapist scaled Steven's confidence level on 1 to 10 [highest confidence] and Steven replied that he was at 10. The following brief dialogue shows how realistic Steven's scale was.)

Therapist: How do you know that 10 is happening?

> *Steven: I'm not scared today. I feel calm today.*
> *Therapist: If I'd asked you that same scale on Friday,*
> *   where would you put yourself?*
> *Steven: I'd say 2.*
> *Therapist: Why not 1 or 0?*
> *Steven: I was hyper, but I didn't go into the hospital.*
> *Therapist: How did you stay at a 2?*
> *Steven: Taking the advice.*

Even in the midst of a very scary situation, Steven's ability to track and his ability to think things through was intact and his scale was quite realistic.

Steven appeared before the judge accompanied by the network of supportive people he had created for himself. This included his sister, the pastor of his church and members of the congregation, and some of the River Club staff and his friends at the club. The court eventually ordered him to a psychiatric examination at the county clinic with the possibility of ordering him into inpatient care for 90 days. We were concerned that, given Steven's past history, the evaluating psychiatrist would recommend inpatient treatment, but Steven reported that, while he was very anxious about this, he did very well in the interview and the psychiatrist's opinion was that inpatient treatment was not necessary. The judge ordered the charges to be dropped, with the condition that Steven stay out of trouble.

I discussed the outcome with Steven and asked him how he thought this happened. Steven said that much to his surprise he wasn't nervous and was able to talk to the psychiatrist logically and calmly. Steven was proud of how he was able to talk to the judge in court and assure him that he had learned his lesson.

A major test of Steven's progress came in the spring of 1998 when his mother died of long-standing heart disease. The social supports he had developed over the past two years were extremely helpful in getting him through this difficult period. Again, Steven reported that he didn't even think about checking into the hospital and credited a large network of family, River Club staff and members, church pastor and members, and medication. Nevertheless, he certainly was sad and worried about how he was going to take care of himself and where he would live, because he

had never lived on his own. Based on the progress that he had
made so far, Steven's sister Evelyn invited him to live with her and
her children.

Steven continued to attend River Club, received medication from
the clinic, and increased his work hours in the River Club job program. He continued to be active in his church, to be helpful to his
sister and nieces, and to go to the library when he had time. He
further reduced the frequency of his appointments with me. The
following is an excerpt from his termination interview, which we
conduct routinely.

> Interviewer (Janet Campbell): What happened here that
>   was helpful for you?
> Steven: I first started coming June 7, 1996. As soon as I
>   started coming here, I started doing better. In the other
>   therapy, they started getting too personal. I like coming
>   here.
> Janet: Is there anything we missed that we could have done
>   better?
> Steven: No, everything was just right.
> Janet: Now it's your chance to scale the therapist you
>   worked with. On a scale of 1 to 10, where would you
>   put him?
> Steven: 10.
> Janet: What put him there?
> Steven: The way he expressed things. He helped me to un-
>   derstand better.
> Janet: If a friend or family member asked you to describe
>   what happened here, what would you tell them?
> Steven: When I first started coming, I was nervous. But af-
>   ter a couple of weeks, I started feeling really different. It
>   helped out really good. They really helped me here.
> Janet: Any other comments?
> Steven: I made a lot of progress over the last two years.

The team and I worked with Steven for approximately two years
and five months for a total of 18 sessions. Since the end of my
work with Steven, I have left the clinic, but Janet Campbell still

works there half-time. Steven has requested two brief sessions with Janet "just to stay on track." He has asked about me and told Janet to relay the message to me that he is doing well. Steven still comes to the clinic for his medication check and supply once every two months and continues to participate in River Club four days a week. Now, two years after our therapy ended, Steven still works in the job program of River Club and is doing quite well. I am very pleased that Steven achieved his most important goal: to stay out of the hospital. I am thankful to Steven for making this world a little better place by having touched my professional life. I am confident that his caring and supportive family and friends think the same.

Simon's and his team's work with Steven over the span of two years and five months for the total of 18 sessions can be viewed as brief therapy, as a minimalist approach to working with such heavy-duty problems. The team stayed the course of solution-building during several defining events in Steven's recovery process, never losing sight of what he wanted. Remarkably, Steven never gave up on himself, except the brief hospitalization after his father's death. The team and the therapist maintained their faith in his ability to make the right choices under stress. What a contrast to how other mental health professionals had seen him over many years of psychiatric "care."

This story also shows the typical therapeutic process of "two steps forward and one step back," especially when working with clients like Steven with heavy diagnostic labels. Each "step back" is viewed as a learning process, an opportunity to discover what to do more of, not as a disaster or indication of deeper trouble with the therapy or the client. No matter what "setback" Steven experienced, Simon stayed focused, helping Steven fine-tune his movement forward toward his goals.

Much research as well as common sense shows that people with severe mental illness do better when they are surrounded by a supportive social network, and Steven is a good example of that. We also find that many clients who complain of "hearing voices" report that when they are talking to other people or keeping busy, they hear the voices less often or become less distracted by them.

It makes sense that the more isolated anyone is, the more likely he is to exhibit symptoms. Once again, we are reminded that we are social beings and we function best in a supportive environment.

We particularly like the therapist's question "How are you helping the medication work for you?" It presupposes that the management of the symptom is under the guidance and control of the client, rather than the other way around. Surprisingly, a large number of clients respond as Steven did, achieving more and more control over their lives when given the responsibility and tools to do so. Unfortunately, convincing clients that they can take control of their lives often takes a very long time: Many sessions of solution talk are needed to counteract the years of negative messages that they were out of control and that only someone else or something else (like medication) could control them.

Schizophrenia is a label for a condition often associated with (and, unfortunately, worsened by) despair and hopelessness on the part of the client and apathy and frustration on the part of the professionals. I was impressed with the very respectful way the therapist in this case used SFBT scaling and questions in the context of a caring conversation to kindle hope and support new and rewarding changes in Steven's life.

The therapist particularly showed respect in the way he chose to give Stephen "process" compliments rather than "evaluative" compliments. For example, an evaluative compliment like "that took courage," communicates that the therapist is making a positive evaluation of the client's behavior. This implicitly puts the therapist in a dominant position, and could even be interpreted as gratuitous or patronizing when addressed to a person who has spent extended time in the "inferior" social position of being a psychiatric patient. Instead, asking Steven "How did you find the courage to tell her?" places Steven in the empowering expert position of choosing or not choosing to help the therapist understand how he found courage.

CONCLUSION

Collecting these stories has been a labor of love and sheer pleasure for us both. We have been moved and touched by each and every story. Sometimes we broke out into silent smiles in response to a story. Other times we spontaneously laughed out loud. And with some stories we had to pause and use several tissues to wipe away our tears.

The process of collecting and sorting through these stories deepened our appreciation of how gifted therapists and remarkable clients use language as the primary creative tool to transform the mundane straw of life's burdens and problems into the gold of unique and meaningful solutions for a more satisfying existence. In reading and rereading the stories we noticed how careful each therapist had been to sort out which straws of the client's information had the most potential for becoming a gold thread of solution and which did not.

Once again we realized how much is required from the therapist in order to accomplish this. In order to succeed, the therapists had to exhibit not only a high degree of clinical skill, but also heightened sensitivity to the subtle nuances of language that signal therapeutic potential. It takes considerable wisdom, maturity, and discipline to pull out golden straws of exceptions from a haystack of general information.

In all of the stories, it was the client who supplied the initial raw ingredients and the overall pattern needed to weave together a satisfying and effective solution. Depending upon the client's preferences and availability of additional therapy team members, sometimes one, two, or several more people collaborated to come up with the necessary technological expertise to ensure that the resulting solution tapestry would be not only appealing to the client but practical and long-lasting as well.

Even after all these years, we are still amazed at the virtually alchemical properties of language: how talking becomes the primary tool to spin the straw of problems into the gold of exceptions, solutions, and ultimately a more satisfying quality of life. The particular kinds of questions a therapist asks, the meaning he or she implies, hints at, or embodies all further contribute to the process of spinning solutions. While the situations described in the stories varied considerably, you may have noticed a common thread that distinguishes SFBT from traditional problem-solving approaches. Every therapist you met in these pages demonstrated a posture of gentle thoughtfulness, reverence for the client's wishes, and respectful desire to restore the client's dignity in the least intrusive and most empowering manner possible. By gently directing the flow of conversation, each therapist repeatedly created practical and compelling opportunities for the client to uncover or rediscover resources and strengths that had been previously hidden from view.

We hope that you, too, will join us in this magical process of linguistically spinning straw into gold.

Insoo Kim Berg
Milwaukee, Wisconsin

Yvonne Dolan
Denver, Colorado

REFERENCES

Anderson, H., & Goolishian, H. (1992). The client is the expert: A not-knowing approach to therapy. In S. McNamee & K. J. Gergen (Eds.), *Therapy as social construction*. Newbury Park, CA: Sage.

Cantwell, P., & Holmes, S. (1994). Social construction: A paradigm shift for systemic therapy and training. *Australia and New Zealand Journal for Family Therapy, 15*(1), 17–26.

DeJong, P., & Berg, I. K. (1998). *Interviewing for solutions*. Pacific Grove: Brooks/Cole.

de Shazer, S. (1985). *Keys to solution in brief therapy*. New York: Norton.

de Shazer, S. (1998). *Words were originally magic*. New York: Norton.

Lipchik, E. (1999). Theoretical and practical thoughts about expanding the solution-focused approach to include emotions. In W. R. Ray & S. de Shazer (Eds.), *Evolving brief therapy: In honor of John Weakland* (pp. 157–177). Galena, IL: Geist and Russell.

McLeod, W. (1986). Stuffed team members. *Dulwich Centre Review*. Adelaide, Australia: Dulwich Centre.

Miller, G., & de Shazer, S. (2000). Emotions in solution-focused therapy: A re-examination. *Family Process, 39*(1), 5–23.

LIST OF CONTRIBUTORS

Sverre Barth, M.D.
Finnhaugveien 7
N-0751 Oslo, Norway

John Briggs
Solutions Behavioral Health Group
Milwaukee, Wisconsin
t: (414) 7677-0740
e: johnbriggs@aol.com

Karl Butinga
Hogeschool, Netherlands

Bernie Carter
e: melbernie@earthlink.net

Melissa Darmody
Brief Therapy Team
Dublin, Ireland

Dorothy (Dotty) Decker
M.S.W., D.C.S.W., L.M.F.T.
409 Plymouth Road, Suite 150
Plymouth, Michigan 48170
t: (734) 455-1880
e: d.h.decker@juno.com

Kotaro Fujioka, M.D.
Shizuoka, Japan
e: fwga6581@ibm.inforweb.ne.jp
or dopey@mb.infoweb.ne.jp.

Jüergen Hargens
Norderweg 14
D-24980 Meyn, Germany
e: juergenhargens@t-online.de

Keizo Hasegawa
mkdm@msj.biglobe.ne.jp

Aviva Holmqvist
Malmo, Sweden
e: aviva@euromail.se

Aviva Homqvist, in private
practice, is a trainer, supervisor,
and consultant to various social
service, criminal justice, and
educational programs.

Tahira Iqbal
Oslo, Norway

Luc Isebaert, M.D., Chief
Dept. of Psychiatry and
Psychosomatic Medicine
St. John's Hospital
Brugge, Belgium

Kikuko Isogai
Fukuoka Brieftherapy
Institute
e: ki_ko@mx5.nisiq.net

Harry Korman, M.D.
e: hkorman@sbbs.se

Jacek Lelonkiewicz
Lodz, Poland
e: jlelon@free.polbox.pl

Anne Lutz, M.D.
Newton, MA

Alasdair Macdonald
e: ajmacdon@psysft.freeserve.co.uk

Robin McCarthy
FamilyWorks
95 India Street
Portland, Maine 04101
f: (207) 773-7213

Daniel Mentha
Jagerstrasse 21
3074 Muri, Switzerland
t/f: 031-952-7003

Marika Moisseeff
Paris, France
e: moisseef@attglobal.net

Janet Roth, doctoral candidate
Brisbane, Australia
e: feathertop@hotmail.com

Britta Severin
Avenbokens Oppenvard
Avenboksgatan 5
231 61 Malmo, Sweden
t: 040-345921
e: solution@malmo.se

John Sharry
Dublin, Ireland
e: johnsharry@binet.ie

Baruch Shulem
Jerusalem, Israel
e: shulemb@netmedia.net.il

Joel K. Simon
7 Ivy lane, Walden, NY 12586
e: joelsim@frontiernet.net

Therese Steiner, M.D.
Zurich, Switzerland
e: steinertheres@pop.agri.ch

Lance Taylor
e: ltaylor@telusplanet.net

INDEX